ADRIFT IN THE STORMS

A Twenty Year Journey to Peace

By

LeAnn Thieman

Published by

Priority Publishing

Colorado

Adrift in the Storms

This book is dedicated to MaiLy.

Her faith, courage, and perseverance

are inspirations to us all.

INTRODUCTION

In *This Must Be My Brother,* LeAnn Thieman recounted her daring adventure of helping to rescue 300 orphans as Vietnam was falling to the Communists. Now, in *Adrift in the Storms,* she tells the true life-story of one orphaned little girl's heroic journey.

Most names in this memoir, as recalled by Maily, have been changed to honor privacy. Some characters are composites of several persons.

Poignant and unforgettable, *Adrift in the Storms: A Twenty Year Journey to Peace* is an inspiration not only to adoptees and their families, but to all learning the true meaning of family.

CHAPTER 1

Denver, Colorado, 1981

Sixteen-year-old MaiLy slammed the door as hard as she could, hoping the beveled glass would break.

"I'm running away for good this time! You'll never see me again!" she screamed, smearing tears from her cheeks.

"I'll show them," she panted. "I ran before and I can run again!" As her bare feet beat against the sidewalk, she relived the night she had run six years ago; the night Vietnam and her life were blown apart.

"MaiLy! My-y-y- Le-e-e-! Wake up, little one!" the nun had said in a frantic whisper. MaiLy had rubbed her sleepy eyes with the back of her hand. "Wake! Hurry!" Sister Katrine gripped her arm and pulled her to a sitting position. "It's time!"

Time for what? Mai wondered as she obediently stood beside the bed and watched Sister wake the other nine-year-old girls in the same way. She shoved them toward Mai, then toward the door and into the black March night. Explosions sounded in the distance. Whimpering children from the other cottages stumbled past her down the dirt path. Minh, her best friend, grabbed Mai's hand and pulled her along through the darkness.

"What's wrong? Where are we going?" Mai's bare feet beat against the earth.

"We're leaving," Minh answered before a nun's voice hissed, "Quiet!"

The score of youngsters was herded to the main gate of the orphanage where they shivered in silence. Clouds blocked the moon and stars that normally provided a peaceful calm. They heard the familiar rumble of Vietnamese army vehicles then gunfire blasts nearby. Huddling closer, they wrapped their arms around each other as tanks thundered through the streets of Dalat and past their gate. The vibration shook through their bones. Mai longed for the familiar tranquilizing sounds of the church bell's toll she had heard just the day before. Instead, gunshots rang in the air, replacing the usually melodious sound of the nuns' choir.

Repeated gunfire blazed sudden bursts of light against the pitch-black curtain of night, as the explosions grew nearer. The trembling children cried softly. Sister Katrine opened the gate a few inches.

"The war is here, my children. Do not be afraid. God will save us but we must hurry to safety now." She pulled two of the older boys from the group and commanded them to run to the convent at the top of the hill. "You are not to stop for any reason." She patted their backs and forced a smile, then nudged them out of the gate. "Run!"

The remaining children looked at one another, their faces streaked with tears. "No! I want to stay here," one boy pleaded.

"Will we come back?" another's voice quaked.

"You must be brave, and run very fast," the nun answered as she coaxed them through the open gate.

Two by two the frightened children ran the half-mile to the convent as the bombing erupted directly outside the fence. Shouts of soldiers and screams of townspeople accompanied the sounds of constant gunfire.

"MaiLy. Minh." Sister placed her hands on their shoulders and forced them to the gate.

"No! No!" Minh begged as Sister shoved them through.

"Come." Mai gripped her hand harder. "Run!"

Minh resisted, pulling back, trying to free her hand from Mai's. Just then a bomb exploded in the street and Minh screamed and ran furiously, breaking Mai's hold.

"Wait!" Mai hollered. "Wait for me!" A second explosion lit the sky and hurled Mai into a run. Her bare feet pounded the trembling earth. Men and women raced across her path, dragging their squalling children behind them as soldiers fired randomly into the fleeing mass.

"Run! Run! Run!" Mai commanded herself, echoing the words of the nun.

More bombs exploded like fireworks, providing the only light as Mai stumbled along the rocky path. She paused a moment at the roadside, heaving and crying and looking for Minh. With both hands over her ears, she shook her head to block the sounds of the deafening detonations. Plopping onto a mound of dirt, she stared into the jungle thicket -- and into the eyes of a soldier whose faced was smeared with the colors of his helmet. He raised his gun and fired over her head.

Mai cried out and jumped to her feet but could not see the path or direction to run. Another blast of the soldier's weapon lit the road where the gun's victim lay bleeding from a gaping chest wound. Mai shrieked and ran past him toward the convent. The sky became brighter as the bombing increased, but smoke clouded her path. She tried to suppress the sobs that spent her diminishing breath.

Tripping, she fell to the ground, her face sliding into the dirt. As she sat up to brush herself off she saw what had caused her to stumble. An arm! Only an arm still in the camouflaged sleeve. She bolted to her feet, screaming, and resumed her race.

"Run! Run! Run!" she repeated to herself. Her tears tasted like dirt, as she wiped them with her grimy hands. Her eyes stung from the billowing smoke and she rubbed them as she darted along the path. When she gasped for breath, the smoldering air filled her head and chest. She covered her mouth to cough and pressed her forearm against the ache in her side.

The convent fence was in sight. Extending her right hand, her fingers bumped against each rail, leading her to the building.

She ascended the stairs two at a time. Sister Katrine was there, waving her into a dimly lit classroom. The tables were pushed to the side and in the corner crouched a dozen frightened children, including Minh. Mai ran to her friend and clung to her.

When the last of the children arrived, the nuns gathered them together to pray. "God will save us," Sister Katrine repeated. Mai didn't believe the smile on the nun's face. She had never seen fear there before.

"I think we might die here," Mai cried to Minh.

The rumbling of the bombing shook the classroom windows and the children.

Sister had to shout to be heard above the mortar's shrill. "Sing, children!" she demanded as she led them in their favorite song.

Meekly, the small voices choked the lyrics, in discordant unison. Another explosion blew out the windows. Terrified sobs replaced the melody.

"Sing!" the nun ordered, raising her shaking hand as if she were directing them in music class. The quivering voices obediently joined her in one more verse of "God Is My Savior".

Hours passed. "Rest," the nuns coaxed. But any attempts to sleep were shattered by the noise of the relentless bombing.

Then Sister Chantel, who was always in charge, turned the lights out and yelled, "Quiet!" Mai heard the roar of an engine and remembered the army tank she had seen shooting people on the road. The nun opened the door a crack and peaked out.

"Come! Hurry!" she shouted, motioning to the children. Dutifully they hustled to the wide-open door. A large army truck sat at the foot of the stairs. Mai froze when she saw a soldier waving them down the steps with a huge gun strapped across his shoulder. She felt a push from the nun behind her.

"Go! Get in!"

The soldier pulled back the canvas canopy and boosted the orphans in two and three at a time. When the benches on the sides were full, the remaining children stumbled in and crowded together on the floor. The two nuns squeezed in beside them, the canvas flap was lowered, and the truck took off with a jerk, jostling its passengers into one another. In the blackness, Mai groped for Minh's hand and cuddled closer to her. The nuns draped blankets over their heads and bodies. The motion of the truck rocked Mai into a fitful sleep as she wondered if she would ever see her orphanage home again.

LeAnn Thieman

CHAPTER 2

The sleepy orphans bumped against each other when
the truck brakes screeched, bringing the vehicle to an abrupt
halt. The driver's door slammed and he came to the back and
lifted the canvas flap. Sounds of distant bombing interrupted
the tranquil glimmer of dawn. Worried children cautiously
hopped out of the truck and onto the deserted road. As they
gazed at the lush vegetable plantations nestled between the
hills, they smiled, believing they had left the danger of the
war behind.

So why did Sister Katrine still look so worried, Mai
wondered.

The fresh morning breeze was a welcome change from
the musty air inside the truck, and the glow of the sunrise
filled the children with enthusiasm. They ran and skipped
around the truck until Sister Chantel directed them to the
fields at the side of the road to pick ripe tomatoes and
cabbages. She held her long apron in front of her, forming a
basket for the collected produce. The boys and girls darted
playfully between the rows, enjoying their new freedom.

But their frivolity was soon interrupted by the sounds of approaching engines and shouts of the driver motioning them into the back of the truck. Sister Chantel bundled the apron of vegetables with one hand as she ran, shooing the children with the other. The little ones clambered into the truck and obeyed the commands to be silent as it sped off.

They traveled all day through sloping terrain, nibbling on rationed portions of collected produce. The groaning gears of the truck and the increasing heat inside made rest difficult. Mai raised the edge of the canvas to peer out, welcoming the puffs of fresh, cooler air on her clammy face. She noticed the road was becoming more crowded, and then felt the slap of Sister's hand on hers. The canvas fell shut and Mai whined as she rested her head on Minh's shoulder while the truck lurched along its route.

By mid-afternoon, the heat inside the rolling tent caused the children to complain as they pulled at damp clothes and mopped sweaty faces with shirtsleeves. The rationed sips of water provided little relief. Smells of perspiration and urine permeated the stagnant, stuffy air shared by too many.

Traffic came to a near-halt. This time, Sister Chantel raised the tarp a few inches and looked out. Hundreds of vehicles crowded the narrow streets.

"We are nearing Nha Trang," she said to Sister Katrine. "No one will notice us here or be suspicious of us." Together they raised the canvas sides of the truck and tied them near the top support bar.

The children smiled and fanned the air toward their faces. When the truck stopped in a traffic jam, they stood, stretched, and allowed the breeze to dry the backs of their clothing.

The two-lane road was congested with six lanes of noisy, disorganized traffic leading to the coastal town. As the truck inched its way toward the city, the crowds grew denser.

7

"DaNang fell to the Communists last week," Sister Chantel explained. "Hundreds of thousands of refugees have fled."

Mobs of frightened civilians choked the dusty district roads and coastal highways. Trucks piled high with baskets and furniture had fifty to sixty people in the rear. One had that many in back and five sitting on the hood. A three-wheeled Lambretta taxi designed for eight people carried sixteen. When a wheel fell off, everyone abandoned the cart in the middle of the crowded highway and set out on foot. Buffalo carts, bicycles, Hondas, and pushcarts were loaded with people and their possessions. Horns honked, tires screeched, and people yelled as they made their way through the coiled serpent of traffic. Men and women carried yokes on their shoulders, with baskets and bags filled with their worldly goods. Their faces were as worn and drab as their tunic-style clothing.

The congestion on the roads was only a sample of what they were to find in Nha Trang, the coastal destination of countless of thousands of refugees. Families sat on mats at the roadside with small kettles sitting atop a tiny clump of burning sticks. They sipped tea and nibbled on the small quantity of food they were able to carry with them on their trek to freedom. Tarps hanging from feeble poles provided makeshift lean-tos.

Sister Chantel, Sister Katrine, and the children huddled close as the truck crept through the panicking chaos in the city. They had been told that churches and schools provided shelter for many refugees. When they saw a distant steeple, they knocked on the cab of the truck and waved their arms to point the driver in that direction.

They were within a few blocks of the church when the driver stopped the truck, got out, and approached Sister Chantel. The noise of the city drowned their voices as they argued. Shortly, Sister turned to her fleeing family and announced that they would get off the truck and walk the remainder of the way. Hesitantly, the children climbed from the back clinging to the nuns' habits. The truck sat trapped in traffic while the Sisters and their charges began the uphill trek to the church. Mai clung to Minh's hand as the children formed a human chain weaving their way past sidewalk shelters and shanties.

"Hold tight," the nuns called as they guided their flock through the throngs of anxious refugees.

Suddenly the earth rumbled with the sound of distant explosions. The mob pushed harder with undisguised panic. Mai and her friends cried, realizing they had not escaped the war that had threatened them the night before. They fought to maintain their grips on each other's hands as the crowd tried to separate them.

They arrived at the church as a second explosion formed a black cloud on the far horizon. Sister Katrine herded the tearful youngsters into the sanctuary while Sister Chantel placed a hand on each of their heads, taking count. Hundreds of people crowded inside in a whispering chorus of fear.

Sister Chantel found an empty row of pews. "We must kneel and thank God for our safe journey," she instructed. Willingly, the children knelt and bowed their heads. Sister Katrine was at Mai's side and gently took her hand as they prayed. Rising, Sister Chantel approached a group of men in business suits. One man gestured with his hands as he talked above the expected whisper. They talked a long time before Sister shook his hand gratefully, and returned to share his news with Sister Katrine.

"We are indeed blessed, Sister," she began. "Dalat fell to the Communists this morning. Hundreds of troops have been deployed to prevent the exodus of people from the Central Highlands to the coast. We are very fortunate to have made it here. Over 50,000 people are detained in a roadblock between the river and the communists. The man I spoke to is a government official. He says refugee columns are being harassed again and again by enemy fire. There have been heavy casualties."

Sister Katrine shook her head and made the sign of the cross as she listened.

"The Vietcong are heading here, to Nha Trang," Sister Chantel continued. "We can only pray that our troops can stop them."

"I have been thinking," Sister Katrine began cautiously. "Thinking and praying," she added. "I want to take MaiLy to the coast and try to get her to Saigon, to the Masons."

Sister Chantel was shaking her head. "Absolutely not!" she hissed. "We must stay together!"

"But Mother Superior," Sister Katrine pleaded, "there is no reason not to try now."

"You could both die trying!" the older nun almost shouted.

"And we could both die here," Sister Katrine said emphatically. "The Masons have loved her and waited for her for seven years. You know we have not always been fair or honest with them. Yes, we prayed Mai would go to France and become a nun, but there is no chance for that now. Let me try to give her one last chance for happiness."

"No, we must stay together," Sister Chantel repeated.

Sister Katrine paused, her head low. "I am taking MaiLy," she said softly. Then looking into her superior's eyes she repeated aloud, "I am taking Mai."

Sister Chantel looked shocked by this insubordination.

"With or without your consent, Mother Superior, but I pray you will give me your blessing."

Sister Chantel shook her head slowly, and then said, "Where will you go? What will you do?"

"I am not sure," the nun admitted, "but God will guide me. I must find a way to Saigon. There I will find the agency that the Masons work with."

They stood in silence. "I must try," was all Sister Katrine could add.

"God be with you," Sister Chantel said as she placed Mai's hand in Sister Katrine's. Reaching into the deep pocket of her habit, she removed some money and pressed it into Sister Katrine's hand. "This is not much, but it is all we can spare." Then, bending down, she hugged Mai for the first time. Mai stood stiffly, unsure how to respond. "Go with Sister Katrine, MaiLy. Follow her, and always follow God."

Mai looked at the tears in the nun's eyes then gently planted a kiss on the damp cheek. Sister Chantel smiled and stood. "Go, then," she said in her usual stern voice, "before dark."

"Thank you." Sister Katrine squeezed the nun's hand. "And God bless you and the children." With that, she took Mai's hand and led her to the doorway, down the stairs, and into the chaos of the street. MaiLy looked back at the church.

No time for good-byes.

CHAPTER 3

With the setting sun to her back, Sister Katrine gripped Mai's hand and raced east toward the shore. She knew her only hope for escape lay in an ocean attempt. Sister Chantel's report of ground troops harassing and firing on refugees shattered any plan to get south to Saigon by land.

Swarms of people raced through the streets with increased intensity and panic. Sister took her rope belt and tied it around Mai's waist, then her own. She wiped a tear from the child's cheek and silently resumed her pace. Sounds of distant gunfire fueled the terrorized throngs. Fleeing refugees mixed with armed troops. Streets were so jammed with bicycles, honking trucks, and moaning oxen that all movement was halted.

Sister Katrine spun around, gazing in all directions. Then mobs forced her and Mai to move with the civilian stampede that knocked street vendor tables to the ground. A woman lay over the body of her fallen child, protecting her from the trampling horde.

An old woman shrieked as the little boy she was carrying fell from her arms and rolled in front of a passing cart. Sister Katrine instinctively lurched for the child and swept him into her arms as the wagon raced by. Mai had been jerked to the ground but suppressed her own tears as she watched the old woman embrace the rescued toddler. Over and over the feeble woman thanked Sister Katrine for saving the boy.

"Follow me," she said as she led them to a narrow alley. "I will show you safe passage." Sister and Mai followed as she wound her way through the crowded back streets of the city. Every doorway was packed with people. Smells from overturned garbage containers mixed with odors of foods being cooked at street-side camps. Sounds of screaming people intensified with each burst of distant thunder as the ground rumbled. Periodically, the old woman stopped to lean on a building, her wrinkled face ashen, her respirations labored. Sister put an arm around the frail body and helped her along until she was steady again.

Finally their guide stopped at a shanty and greeted a family huddled before a small open flame. She introduced her daughter, son-in-law, and two of their young children. The younger woman eased her mother into a makeshift chair near the fire.

The matriarch smiled, then took her daughter's hand while she relayed the account of Sister Katrine's heroic rescue of their child. Bowing from the waist before the nun, the couple stammered words of appreciation then insisted Sister and Mai share their meager meal and sleep on their mats next to the street.

Sister untied Mai from her waist tether, but Mai stayed cuddled at her side. She ate eagerly with her bare hands and listened as the adults talked about the plan for tomorrow-- the plan to escape to Saigon. The man had worked for the United States government there. Rumors predicted all nationals who had assisted the U.S. would be killed or put in prison camps if the Communists defeated South Vietnam.

"For a decade I have worked to help my country; now I am forced to flee from it." The man spoke sadly as he sipped his drink. "Our only hope is to get to Saigon and the U.S. Embassy to escape to the United States. The American that I worked for promised we would be taken care of because I aided the American efforts so loyally."

Their voices faded as Mai curled up on a straw mat next to Sister Katrine and drifted asleep.

The smell of rice and fish simmering in a pot woke her the next morning. She was relieved to see Sister Katrine still at her side, diapering a baby. Sister smiled when she saw Mai's sleepy eyes open, and gently patted her back.

"Where are we going?" Mai finally asked. "I don't want to stay here. I am afraid."

"We are going to a big city called Saigon," the nun answered as she dressed the child she was tending. "I want to help you get to America, to the Masons." Mai didn't understand what she meant, but there was no time to explain as the meal was served, then the mats rolled up for travel.

The family packed all they had into a bag on the father's shoulders. The mother strapped one child to her front and another to her back. The old woman lugged the toddler she had carried the day before, and the group trekked east with Sister Katrine and Mai following.

They walked for hours in 100 degree heat, through legions of refugees hauling their life's' possessions. At first Mai wondered why all the people were running, but the convoy of tanks rumbling down the streets, splitting the crowds, answered her unspoken question. Her legs grew tired as she hustled alongside Sister Katrine, again tied to the nun's robe. She longed for her sandals. Occasionally, they stopped to share sips of warm water and allow the grandmother to rest before resuming their frantic pace. Sister Katrine's heavy white veil cropped her red sweaty face as she helped carry the toddler and support the old woman.

By midday, Mai could smell the salty fresh breeze of the ocean. Soon the soft sand of the beach caressed her swollen bare feet. She longed to sit and play in the sand, but

Sister pulled her along. The yelling and fighting of the tens of thousands of people flooding the beach drowned out the sounds of waves rippling to shore. Several cargo ships had docked and multitudes of refugees deluged the area, begging to get on board. Soldiers fired their guns over the crowd in futile attempts to stop them, but the sounds of gunfire only seemed to heighten the fury. Men shoved women and children out of the way to fight for a place in line. Soldiers threw down their guns and jumped on board. Citizens waved fistfuls of money, knowing that was the ultimate guarantee for transport. Others tried to sell their precious family heirlooms for a chance for freedom.

Mai and Sister Katrina followed their host family to a less crowded part of the shoreline where they met another family building a raft. The adults shook hands and made necessary introductions. The man who seemed to be in charge of the raft's construction glared at Mai and Sister, shaking his head. Wheezing, the old lady told him about Sister Katrine rescuing the toddler. Grumbling, he went back to work.

Sister led the venerable woman and MaiLy to a nearby palm tree. She made a mat from fallen branches for them to rest upon. The enfeebled woman managed a faint smile, her blackened teeth telling of her many years chewing the betel nut. Mai knew the nut juice provided energy for work in the sun, and only active, strong-minded women enjoyed the habit. Now the exhausted laborer slowly closed her eyes. Mai remained with her, tenderly holding her hand and offering her sips of water when she woke, coughing.

Sister joined the construction crew, taking her place alongside men rolling tree trunks in a row. She pushed her sleeves to her elbow, ignoring their baffled looks as she maneuvered a log.

Hours passed and the afternoon sunset promised relief from the sweltering heat. Mai didn't leave the side of the ailing old woman, but clung to her hand for mutual support. She watched as the men pushed the tethered raft offshore and cheered as it bounced atop the small waves. They pulled it back to the beach then frantically began to organize the other family members and their belongings. There was much bickering as some sacks were put on the raft and others tossed back onto the sand. Mai counted three men, three women and five children taking turns sitting on various areas of the eight-foot raft with their parcels tied to its edges. She smiled as she watched Sister Katrine working with her long habit dragging in the water.

The shadows of dusk crept over the land when Sister went to the palm tree to get Mai and the old woman. Mai pulled on the woman's bony brown hand to help her to stand, but it took Sister's arms around her to get her to her feet. She moaned as she started to walk. Mai coaxed her along. The thirty paces to the water's edge seemed to drain all the strength and breath from the increasingly frail matron. Her daughter and son-in-law jumped off the raft and each took an arm to help her aboard.

"No," the old woman said standing firm. Her daughter looked at her in disbelief. "I am too old and too tired for this journey."

"No, no, no," her daughter said, putting her arm around her to lead her on board. "We are in great danger here."

The old woman pulled back. "They will not hurt an old woman like me. I will return to our home to guard the spirit of our ancestors." She gestured toward the moon peeking over the horizon. "The moon is full. I must place flour, money, and fruit before the family shrine and burn incense there. I will honor our ancestors until I join them."

The daughter stood staring into the wrinkled face, then kissed the leather-like brown skin stretched across bony cheeks. She clutched the hands that had bathed, fed, spanked, and caressed her.

"Please don't make me leave you, Mama." She squeezed the skeletal hands in hers.

"Please don't make me go," her mother wheezed.

They stood staring into each other's eyes until someone on the raft shouted they must leave on the outgoing tide.

The old woman touched her daughter's ears. "Since you were a little girl I have told you your long Buddhist ear lobes mean you will have a long and fruitful life. Go now and live it."

The young woman threw her arms around her mother and wept. Her husband gently pried her from the maternal embrace and backed her onto the raft as it was pushed from the shore.

Mai and Sister jumped on board and watched the silhouette of the old woman disappear as she hobbled toward the setting sun.

As their rig drifted into the South China Sea, they looked back at a city on fire.

CHAPTER 4

Was it two days? Or had it been three or four that the raft rocked relentlessly over the current. Mai slowly pulled herself into a sitting position and hugged her head as she peered over the edge of the cardboard box where Sister had placed her. Mercifully, sleep had shielded her from much of the seasickness plaguing the other passengers crammed together on the raft.

Sister Katrine put a small bottle of water to Mai's lips but allowed her only a few swallows. Tarps on poles flapped in the wind and provided little relief from the scorching noon sun. Mai slumped back onto the bottom of her cubicle and Sister draped her habit over the top of the box to shade her.

Later Sister used her apron to wipe vomit from Mai's face then rinsed it in the sea.

When Mai woke next, Sister offered her a chunk of bread, taking only a morsel for herself. Mai broke hers again and gave part back to the nun, smiling faintly. Sister returned the grin and they eagerly ate their portions. The food seemed to nurture Mai's spirit as well as her body. She sat up to gaze across endless acres of ocean. Brushing her matted hair from her face, she breathed deeply the salty air. Cloud cover had turned it to a cool wind that relieved the burning she felt inside.

Mai watched as the young mother held her head over the side of the raft and emptied her churning stomach. Her children moaned in unison, as they lay wedged together on the rig.

Mai guessed the rooster in a small bamboo crate would be their next meal, should stomachs settle. As she listened to the chicken cluck his lullaby, she slumped back into her box and daydreamed about her life at the orphanage where she woke daily to the rooster's crow.

Usually she covered her head with her pillow, still damp with last night's tears. But the rooster would relentlessly repeat his wake-up call until Mai's feet dutifully hit the floor. She made her bed quickly but neatly. The uniform she washed the night before wasn't dry, so she dressed in the second identical one. She quickly buttoned the grimy white blouse and pulled the blue plaid jumper over her head. Her brown sandals still looked new, she thought, as she buckled them. Most people assumed she didn't like wearing them since she ran barefoot most of the time. The truth was, she loved them. They were one of the few things she had ever gotten new and she wanted to keep them looking that way. She learned not to run to the nuns when she got small cuts and bruises on her feet because they offered her little sympathy after her barefoot escapades.

Mai pulled back the curtain separating her from her roommates, and smiled at Minh.

A glass doorway separated their quarters from the concrete slab outside. Already the workers were there, filling the metal laundry tubs with water and beginning the chores of the day. Three pigs snorted in the adjacent pen as they gobbled the brown slop a woman dumped in the trough. A dozen hens pecked at their remnants of grain.

Mai had watched ducks being butchered the day before. She winced as she recalled the nuns boiling vats of water then chopping off their heads and plucking feathers from their scalded bodies.

Mai took Minh's hand and they walked to breakfast. When the cooked rice cereal was spooned into her bowl, Mai wrinkled her nose and snorted like a pig. The children at her table tried unsuccessfully to stifle their giggles. She pushed her nose up to form a snout and snorted even louder, dropping her head over her bowl. When she felt the tap of a spoon on her skull, she ended her antics and looked up, relieved to see Sister Katrine. With a wink, Sister reprimanded her, and Mai sat straight and finished her meal.

A clanging bell called her to class where fifteen nine-year-olds sat in obedient silence. As the priest reviewed their French lesson, Mai's mind wandered in a daydream. It wandered past the gates of Domani de Marie and into the vast lands beyond-- beyond the thousands of acres of terraced vegetable gardens; beyond the pine forests, mountain streams and waterfalls; beyond... WHACK. Father's ruler slapped her hand. He repeated the question for what he claimed was the third time, and Mai recited the French assignment she had memorized the night before.

Because it was Saturday, school lasted only a half-day. Usually the afternoon was spent in the fields, but today the work was cut short. The Red Cross workers had come to give immunization shots to every child, followed by large doses of oil gagged down their throats. The entire lot of children cried and coughed and choked until they were finally told they could spend the rest of the day playing. Immediately, the bawling, sputtering group ran outside, cheering.

After changing into their only set of play clothes, the girls began their hopscotch and jump rope routines while the boys played marbles. Mai was usually the hopscotch champion and today was no exception.

Sliced tomatoes made for a refreshing snack before they raced to the gate that separated them from the rest of the world. Breathless, the boys and girls stood quietly listening to the church bells toll. The air breezed past the convent on the hill carrying the aroma of the nuns' fresh baked breads and the melodious harmony of their choir. The world on the other side of the gate seemed to beckon them. Traffic, family outings, and street vendors lured them to that excitement. But soldiers marching with guns slung over their shoulders and sandbag fortresses in the streets warned of danger the children couldn't comprehend. Their safety felt threatened with the occasional passing of an army tank. Every child had been warned not to touch the wires strewn around the area. "Boom!" was the only word of caution and explanation.

Mai stared into the thick forest that bordered one side of the road. Though she couldn't see it, she recalled a cemetery there and shivered as she remembered burying someone in the cool mist of a gray day years ago.

The rest of her companions sauntered back to their cottages but Mai stayed, clinging to the gate, gazing at the world so foreign to her. She sensed that world promised a better life. She fantasized about Pete, the soldier who had spent so much time with her, and wondered if she had misunderstood his vow to return. Many other soldiers had come to visit, all dressed in their camouflage uniforms, but none had touched her heart as he had. She peered though the gate and visualized the day he would come through it and take her away. She wouldn't cry, next time. She would hold his hand, walk through this exit, and never come back.

The sound of the church bell summoned her to Saturday chapel. She ran to the church and took her place in line. The peacefulness inside made it her favorite place. She didn't even mind kneeling in the dark confessional and telling Father her sins. In church she found comfort, acceptance, and an unconditional love.

She went to the front and knelt before the statue of the Virgin Mary. There was a similar sculpture in the entryway of her dormitory. Mai prayed to God through Mary every day. She knew that Jesus had just one woman to care for Him, not many as she did. Along with His mother He had a father.

That was Mai's only wish.

During the Vietnamese New Year holiday, TET, many of the orphans went to stay with townspeople for a day or two. Mai had visited a woman on several occasions that had a son and daughter. Even though things seemed unhappy there, Mai knew she wanted to be a part of that kinship. In her heart she knew that one-day her prayers would be answered.

But when?

At supper she noticed duck meat had replaced the usual fish in the rice. She tried to erase their slaughter and scalded bodies from her mind as she swallowed hard. There were no choices at mealtime and Sister frequently reminded them how lucky they were to have food because many children were starving, even in Vietnam.

Everyone looked forward to TET, as that was the only time they feasted. The holiday table was covered with baked turkey, roasted duck, Ramen noodle soup, pork, sugar-coated coconut, sticky rice rolled in bamboo leaves, and many other favorites.

But today, rice and dead duck would have to do.

It was Mai's group's turn to do the dishes while the others cleaned the floor. As they paraded to their cottages for bed, Mai paused before the statue of Mary, then walked slowly down the dark hallway to her room. With each step the gloomy corridor stole her joy.

She and Minh took turns brushing each other's hair before bed and chatted about how great it would be when they were twelve and would be allowed to have longer hair.

Until that time, it would remain bobbed just below their ears.

Another clang of the bell and lights were out. The curtains were pulled and Mai knelt at her bedside and prayed before crawling into bed.

In the daytime it was too noisy and at night it was too quiet. For her first four years at the orphanage she had gone to sleep and woken to the sounds of crying babies. Whenever she could, she walked by the nursery and toddler center to hear the crying and felt a strange sense of comfort and lonely belonging.

In the quiet of the night she wiped her eyes with her pillowcase as she hugged and rocked herself to sleep.

The violent rocking of the raft and the cackling of the caged rooster roused Mai from her daydream. A sudden gust of wind ripped the tarp and the men rushed to detach it. The gale persisted causing the raft to lunge madly over the swell. Soon icy waves pounded over the voyagers and their cargo. The deafening roar drowned out hollered commands and prayers. Adults grabbed the squalling soaked children to protect them from the bellowing sea. Mai remained in the box but clung to Sister Katrine as the crest engulfed their vessel, threatening to overturn it. Then a white mountain of water crashed over the raft, slapping Mai's face and filling her lungs with stinging saline. Coughing and gasping for breath, she clamored for Sister Katrine. The cardboard box disintegrated and she rolled to the edge of the raft, stopped by a jolt to her midsection- -Sister Katrine had tied her rope belt around her waist again. While Sister pulled, Mai crawled back to her trembling embrace. With her head on Sister's chest, Mai heard the nun's frantic prayer. For hours, the ruthless waves battered their bodies relentlessly and they fought to keep from being devoured by the monstrous sea.

The sun's slow descent on the horizon seemed to steal the power from the storm. The gentle rain that followed washed the burning salt from their skin and the panic from their hearts. After filling their containers with fresh rainwater, everyone collapsed to rest.

Soaring gulls, against the lustrous red sunset, sang a peaceful promise. A vibrant rainbow arched across the rippling blue water. As their craft rocked gently again, prayers were audible in falling rain.

Only then did Mai begin to whimper. Sister Katrine held her close and whispered, "God protects us from life's storms, MaiLy, then gives us beautiful rainbows. That's His sign He'll take care of you. You'll see."

CHAPTER 5

Denver, Colorado, April 3, 1975

Peter Mason slumped onto the couch and covered his face with his arms while the news announcer detailed the escalation of the Vietnam War and the fall of the city of Dalat to the Communists. His shirtsleeves absorbed his tears. "Where's MaiLy? What's happening to her? She must be scared to death!"

His wife, Connie, sat beside him and wrapped her arms around his chest.

"How will we ever find her now?" he moaned.

"We'll find her," Connie soothed. "After seven years of trying to adopt her, we aren't going to give up now. I'll go make some phone calls to the State Department and to Cherie, in Saigon, and see if I can find out anything more." She kissed his cheek, then left him alone.

"Oh, MaiLy," he whispered, "I know I was supposed to have found you then. Now how can I let you go?"

He lay back on the couch and rested his arm over his forehead and smiled as he relived the first time he had seen her at the orphanage, seven years ago.

When he had heard the old nun's footsteps echoing down the hall, he stood as if at attention, combing his short brown hair with his fingers. Her habit flowed as she approached him and a required smile broke her stern, plaster mask.

His interpreter had recited the rehearsed introduction and explained that Peter was stationed in Dalat with U.S. Military Intelligence. He missed his wife very much and because he adored children, he wanted to help at an orphanage during his yearlong tour.

"You don't look like a soldier," the Vietnamese nun snapped, staring at his civilian clothes. His interpreter, Tran, explained that the Captain never wore a uniform nor carried a gun. Pete produced his military I.D. card and the suspicious look on the nun's face gave way to the required smile again.

"Welcome to Domani de Marie. I am Sister Chantel. Ours is an order of the Sisters of Charity of St. Vincent de Paul. Our headquarters are in France. We have nearly 100 children here, ranging from babies to ten-year-olds. And we can always use help."

She gestured for them to follow her on a tour of the orphanage complex. First they walked through the nursery area where a dozen cribs sat on polished floors. The babies looked extremely healthy, Pete thought, and he watched with admiration as the three Vietnamese women fed and diapered the cooing infants.

When his guide opened the door to the toddler center, Pete smiled. Sounds of two dozen children laughing and playing made his heart do the same. He gazed around the room at the menagerie of preschoolers, all dressed in the same tunic style shirt and pants. Each little girl had hair cut just below her ears with bangs chopped a few inches above her eyebrows. The little boys with nearly shaved heads, all dressed the same.

Peter slowly made his way through the crowded room, trying to absorb all the commotion. He stumbled when he felt a child run into the side of his right leg and cling to it. He looked down and into the face of a little girl he guessed to be about three years old. She smiled up at him, her dark eyes dancing with mischief and merriment. Her chubby cheeks glowed as her smile broadened and she tightened her grip on his leg.

"MaiLy!" the nun scolded and motioned for the child to let go of Pete's leg. She admonished her in Vietnamese, but the little girl shook her head and held tight. When Sister Chantel grabbed her arm and attempted to pull her away, MaiLy only clutched tighter.

"It's all right," Pete said as he reached down and picked the child up into his arms. MaiLy giggled, revealing deep dimples in her cherub cheeks. Patting his face with her hands, she stared deeply into his blue eyes. Transfixed, Pete barely heard the interpreter explain that she had never done anything like this before.

"While she is an active child, and sometimes even ornery," the nun said, "she has never approached a stranger."

"So maybe we're not strangers," Pete muttered giving the little girl a hug. She wrapped her arms around his neck and squeezed tightly, pressing her cheek against his stubbly face.

"Den!" the nun ordered, pulling the child from his arms. The little girl whined and reached to hug him again, but the nun clapped her hands and the child stood pouting as Pete and Tran headed toward the door. Looking back over his shoulder, Pete noticed her watching him leave.

They walked up the hill to the cottages for older children and peered into the classroom filled with girls in blue plaid jumpers with white blouses and the boys wearing blue pants and sweaters. Students turned to the American at the door until the nun cracked her pointer on her desk to summon their attention. Though the decor was bare and drab, Pete complimented Sister on the well-maintained complex.

"That's because of the help of Americans such as yourself," Sister Chantel acknowledged as they walked across the dirt courtyard separating the buildings.

Since he knew no Vietnamese, Pete was sent to the nursery to work where communication was not a needed skill. As an only child, he had almost no experience with little ones, but he and his wife, Connie, had plans for a big family. So far their attempts to conceive had been disappointing, fueling their dream to adopt a child someday. *Connie will have to teach me a lot,* he thought as he fumbled with the baby in his arms. *Hopefully, since she's one of ten children, she'll have experience enough for both of us.*

His awkward efforts at feeding the baby were interrupted by a familiar thump on his leg, and another knee-hug. Looking down, he grinned into MaiLy's smiling face. She clung to his knee as he walked to the crib and placed the baby inside.

"Hi," he beamed, picking MaiLy up.

"Hi," she repeated, patting his face again. Wrapping her legs around his chest and her arms around his neck, she refused to let him put her down. When Pete chuckled, so did she. He sat cross-legged on the floor with her in his lap. They sat silently looking into each other's smiling face. "Who says we can't communicate?"

When the baby began to cry, Pete stood to finish the feeding. As he walked to the crib, MaiLy sat on his foot and clung to his calf for the ride. He pretended to shake his leg, and she giggled and clutched tighter. They continued this game for most of the hour while he assisted the workers with the babies. Then Tran came and reminded him it was time to leave. He pried the foot passenger from his leg.

"Goodbye," he said, hugging her. "I'll be back next week-- and the week after that-- and the week after that."

Mai protruded her bottom lip in a pout he was sure she had practiced. "I'll see you soon," he promised.

Their jeep passed through the gates of the orphanage and into the beautiful streets of Dalat. The French colonial resort city was a haven in a country torn by decades of war. Many generals and country officials spent days off relaxing and recuperating in this picturesque mountain town. It set 5000 feet above sea level, which provided an ideal climate for recreation and the farming of most of the country's fruits and vegetables. The mountain pine and seventy-five degree temperatures were a sharp contrast to the heat of the lowland jungles. Here men and women dressed in their best clothes to stroll through town every Sunday, while men in combat uniforms ran through perilous thicket in adjacent provinces. Dalat claimed the second largest university in Vietnam, a military academy, a monastery, and a nuclear power plant the French had built. Rumor had it that President Teddy Roosevelt had hunted tiger, panther, bear and boar in the wooded mountains.

As the jeep passed by the stately French-looking villas, Pete was reminded that the area had not always been free from the fighting and he couldn't help wondering if it would remain that way. Previous mortar fire had left pockmarks on the exterior of many buildings. Holes in the structures told the tale of the TET offensive of 1968 when the Vietcong had taken over Dalat. U.S. and A.R.V.N. troops had suffered heavy losses reclaiming the area. House-to-house fighting had resulted in many scars that still remained on villas, telling the war stories.

When Pete had first descended the steps of the aircraft and set foot in Vietnam, he sorrowfully admitted that the terrain, heat, and camouflage surroundings were just as he expected. Within two days he was transported to his station in Dalat, and seemingly another world. He was grateful to get to know the country's people and its customs and already he loved both. There were no U.S. combat units in the city, only his small intelligence division. His work as an advisor for the civilian Vietnamese intelligence agency served as a grave reminder that this peaceful community was an integral part of a horrible war. The posting of Vietnamese guards outside his house every night emphasized the fragility of the peace there. Adding to this protection were booby traps, explosive wires, and geese on the perimeter to announce prospective intruders. He had often teased about the "guard geese" but knew they were an important part of his safety.

Pete parked the jeep in front of the small stucco house he shared with two other Americans, his assistant and a CIA agent. He breathed in the pine-scented air and marveled again at the eight-foot poinsettias blooming in the yard. He immediately went to his room and began his daily letter to Connie.

I met the most wonderful little girl today....

CHAPTER 6

The next weekend, Pete let the door slam behind him, sprinted to the jeep, grabbed the roll bar and swung himself into the seat. Boy, was he looking forward to a few days off. It had been an unusually difficult week, filled with decisions and orders that would lead to the capture of many enemy spies. While he was grateful not to be a part of direct combat, he knew his work affected, and likely took, the lives of many men.

This bothered him because he hadn't expected to fall in love with the Vietnamese people and their culture. Their love and acceptance of him surprised him even more. Though they did not share a language, he was becoming good friends with Auhn, a Vietnamese intelligence officer he worked with daily. With few words in common they were able to spend long hours gesturing, stammering and "discussing" many topics, from philosophy to politics to family.

Pete had been unaware that the bond he felt with Auhn was mutual until he had gone to his wedding the week before. He had enjoyed the wedding ceremony immensely,

31

especially since Tran was there to translate for him and explain the rituals and vows. The only American present, he joined the other guests seated at tables at the reception. When the server presented a whole chicken bobbing in a huge pot of broth, Tran explained that someone would be chosen, by the groom, as the guest of honor at the wedding. The head would be chopped off the bird and presented to that esteemed individual. He or she would then ceremoniously bite into the head of the chicken.

Pete tried not to make a face as he asked, "And this is an honor?"

"There is none greater," Tran said solemnly. "It is usually reserved for heads of families or persons of great importance."

Pete held his stomach and faked a smile as the server produced a huge hatchet-like knife and whacked off the chicken's head. Auhn placed it on a silver platter and slowly walked around the room. The guests were immobilized as they anticipated who would be bestowed this great honor. Auhn picked up the head with his bare hands and, smiling, dangled it in front of Pete. Pete kept both hands on his stomach to keep them from instinctively covering his mouth.

After a hushed silence, the crowd burst into applause. Pete faked an even bigger smile as he slowly stood and received the fowl's head in his palm. Tran sat smiling, seemingly eager to translate this one!

"Thank you, Auhn," Pete began, his mind racing. He said he understood the magnitude of this honor and was deeply grateful. He spoke of the brother-like love that he had developed for Auhn and how much he appreciated being selected to share in such a personal part of their tradition.

"Speaking of tradition," Pete went on quickly, his mind still racing. "In my country the father of the bride is a very special person to whom we pay honor. He pays for and hosts the wedding and gives his daughter to the groom. As you have paid tribute to me by sharing your tradition, I would like to pay tribute to you by sharing mine." He handed the chicken's head to the father of the bride. "Please accept this honor on behalf of me and the United States of America."

Tran smirked as he completed the translation. The bride's father nearly exploded with pride as he leapt forward grabbed the chicken head and crunched it into his mouth. Blood and brains colored his broad smile and dripped down his chin. The crowd clapped with fervor.

Later Auhn had thanked Pete for unselfishly sharing the great honor.

"I was happy to, really," Pete assured him.

Yes, he thought as his jeep lumbered along the road, this is becoming more than just a military stint.

As he headed to the orphanage, his heart seemed to join in the tune he was whistling. Mentally, he recited over and over again his last letter from Connie. She was pregnant. Their dreams of having a child would come true in October. His initial sadness of not being with her at he birth was soon replaced with the joy of knowing he was going to be a daddy. In the same letter Connie had reminded him she still wanted to fulfill their other dream to adopt a child and suggested that he look into that while he was in Dalat. "Maybe you could pick our son or daughter while you are there," she had written. Pete shook his head as the jeep bumped along. How could you ever choose a child?

He downshifted the jeep as it climbed the hill to the orphanage. Less than a half-mile from Domani de Marie a huge cemetery blanketed the hillside. Pete shuddered as he recalled the story he'd heard just the day before. During the TET offensive of '68, the Vietcong had entered Dalat through this cemetery on the edge of the thick pine forest. Because the orphanage sat overlooking the city, the Vietcong had taken it over as headquarters. For more than a month the children had hidden in the basement under mattresses. Pete winced as he imagined it. He rubbed his eyes as if to erase the picture of MaiLy and the other children huddled under a mattress, afraid and crying. As he approached the compound's gates he wondered if she would still remember him.

He stopped at the convent and spoke with Sister Chantel. She directed him to the nursery where he began helping the workers wash dirty diapers. Wringing them out the best he could, he then rinsed them in the cold water provided.

He was continually impressed with the nonverbal communication he shared with his native hosts. The worker directed him to a clothesline in the backyard where he hung the laundry in the afternoon sun. He silently admitted that he enjoyed the task and grinned when he imagined doing this for his own baby next year.

A bell clanged and a score of toddlers running into the sunshine filled the yard. Leading the pack was MaiLy. She spotted him immediately and ran to him with her arms outstretched. He squatted to embrace her before   she could grab his leg. He felt her soft arms around his neck and her chubby cheeks pressed against his. A feeling of love fluttered inside him-- one he had not experienced before. Her soft panting breath caressed his neck and only her giggle interrupted the hug. Several other little girls approached, but she swatted them away. Peter laughed and opened his arms to welcome them all.

MaiLy pushed his chin with her hand until he was facing only her again

"Hi!" she said with apparent pride in her mastery of the English language.

"Hi!" Pete chuckled, pleased that she remembered his greeting from his first visit. MaiLy pulled on his hand to signal him to come with her, forcing him to stand and break the hug with the others. She led him to a crude rope swing and motioned for him to sit in it. Then she climbed onto his lap, placed his arms around her waist, and rested her head on his chest. They swung slowly in silence.

He felt that same fluttering feeling inside again.

He photographed the moment in his mind, committing it to memory. After a while he remembered his assignment, gently took MaiLy from his lap, and gestured to the laundry basket. She followed him to the clothesline, then, giggling, sat on his foot and clutched his lower leg as he hung the diapers on the line. Whenever he looked down, she tipped her head back and beamed a smile.

Later that afternoon he arrived at his house, went directly to his room, and began his letter to Connie.

I learned something amazing today. You don't choose a child; she chooses you.

CHAPTER 7

Peter went to the orphanage almost every weekend for the next several months. He enjoyed the maintenance work and playing with the children, but most of all, seeing MaiLy. Each time he went he took photos and sent the film home. Connie wrote that she was developing, not only the pictures, but also a deep love for Mai.

And Mai was developing a love of the camera; striking a pose the instant Pete reached into his bag.

He hadn't known what it was like to love a child, but Mai was teaching him in a hurry. He waited several months before asking Sister Chantel if Mai was available for adoption.

"No!" she almost shouted then lowered her voice to add that none of the children were adoptable. When he asked why, she insisted that the Vietnamese could take care of their own.

"Besides," she added, "MaiLy's birth mother is an important socialite and will likely come to claim her one day." Pete decided not to argue that this story was conflicting with one a younger nun had told him earlier. She had claimed MaiLy's birth mother was a peasant woman who sold vegetables at the market. The father of the child was unknown. Therefore, the baby had been abandoned at the door of the orphanage when she was just a few days old.

Pete knew that in Vietnam "you are who your father is." Families took care of their own when the bloodlines were clear. If not, the child was given away. Pete tried to be patient, but periodically approached Sister Chantel about adopting Mai. Each time she emphatically denied his request.

Once she suggested that he adopt one of the Amerasian children since their people ostracized them. Peter tried to explain that he didn't want just any child- -he wanted Mai. The nun seemed incapable of understanding this and at times seemed suspicious of his motives. Perhaps, Pete thought that was because adoption was not done in Vietnam. There was not even a word for it in their language.

He was shocked when one day, as he pleaded, Sister Chantel said MaiLy was adoptable. The two stories of her mother were false; she had been abandoned at birth.

Pete jumped from his seat and almost hugged the old nun before he stopped himself.

"There is a problem," the nun continued.

There's always a problem, Pete thought.

"There is no agency for adoption in this country. We have no avenues established to facilitate it. That is the real reason why Mai cannot be adopted."

"But if I find a way, can we adopt her?"

"There is no way," Sister Chantel said flatly.

"But if I find a way?" he prodded.

"If you can find a way, yes. But as I said, Captain Mason, there is no way."

"But you don't know my wife," Pete muttered.

Stifling a laugh, he skipped out of the office and went home to write the great news to Connie.

The phone rang in the middle of an October night. Connie was calling from the delivery room to introduce him to his daughter Marcie. Together they cried long distance. He cried with joy at having a baby girl. He sobbed with sorrow that he could not touch her skin or cradle her in his arms or rock her to sleep or watch her suckle from her mother's breast. Little Marcie would be six months old before he could hold her for the first time.

The next day, Sunday, Pete returned to Domani de Marie. He begged the nun to let him take MaiLy on an outing. She said it was out of the question, reminding him that MaiLy had been out of the complex only a few times on planned excursions with the other children. He persisted in his plea until she finally relented.

A short while later, Mai came bounding into the room and his arms, wearing a fancy pink dress.

"Hi!" She radiated the smile of a princess as she fingered the lace and full skirt. Clutching his finger tightly, she strolled beside him down the worn path toward his waiting jeep. As he tried to lead her through the gate, she pulled back and shook her head.

"It's okay," he coaxed, picking her up. He carried her to the jeep and placed her in the seat between him and Tran. Pete had anticipated that she might be a little afraid but felt sure Tran could explain away the worry. She smiled as they slowly accelerated down the road. Pete had dreamed of this day with his future daughter many times and had a perfect plan orchestrated.

They parked downtown and joined the other townspeople strolling the picturesque streets of Dalat. Women in beautiful dresses and sweaters paraded next to men in fine suits. Pete pointed them out to MaiLy and, noticing colorful flowers in the ladies' hair, picked one from the flowerpot and placed it behind Mai's ear.

Pete smiled.

Mai didn't.

A huge lake graced the center of town and a lush green golf course bordered it on one shore. MaiLy walked hesitantly there at his side, her face expressionless.

"She'll cheer up when I implement phase one of my plan for fun," Pete said to reassure himself and Tran. "A paddle boat ride!" he exclaimed to Mai.

She stared back blankly.

The fussing she did as he placed her on the seat was nothing compared to her bawling on board. The harder he paddled and tried to point out the beautiful water or flowers on the beach, the louder she cried. Tran tried in vain to explain they were having fun, but Mai clearly didn't agree.

Pete paddled madly back to the dock then held Mai to his chest as she whimpered.

"Time for phase two of my plan for fun." He smiled into her somber face. "My favorite restaurant on the beach." He was sure she would enjoy her first taste of cola.

But she only cried, refusing to taste it.

When the waiter asked for the third time, "Is everything all right, Sir?" Pete decided it was time to leave.

Thinking it best to skip phase three of his plan, Pete and Tran took Mai back to the orphanage. As soon as she entered the gate, her vivacious smile returned, then she fussed when he had to leave again.

I've got to work on this parenting thing, he thought as he drove away.

The next time I take you from here, MaiLy, it will be to our home and I will be your daddy.

A lonely ache gnawed at Pete's heart as the holiday season approached. He and his American roommates tried to capture the Thanksgiving spirit, but somehow   slicing the turkey with a bayonet spoiled the festive mood.

At Christmas he imagined his wife and daughter at home and found no comfort in the promise of future Christmases with them. He pored over the fistfuls of photos

Connie had sent him of Marcie, but doing so only heightened his homesickness.

Grabbing the small sack of toys he'd bought, he headed to the orphanage where a pine tree, decorated with paper cutouts and pinecones, was the only evidence of the holiday. His melancholy mood was predictably broken when he entered the toddler center and the children flocked around him. Mai shoved the other four-year-olds away and Pete had to gently motion them back. When he shook the bag of toys, they all squealed.

He reached in. "Balloon."

"Balloon," they echoed in unison. Their eyes widened as they watched him blow it up. He tied a knot in the end and batted it to one of the little boys. MaiLy promptly knocked him to the floor, caught the balloon, and proudly returned it to Pete. The little boy began to cry, as did Mai when Pete took the balloon from her and gave it back to him. Pete blew up the entire bag of balloons and tossed them to the children. Soon the room was vibrating with sounds of laughter and trampling feet.

Three nuns entered, all frowning. Taking his cue, Pete gathered the balloons, quieted the youngsters, then shook his sack of toys again. The giggling children clapped their hands and heaved sighs of anticipation.

Their faces reflected disappointment, though, when he pulled out a kazoo. They looked at one another with bewilderment. Pete placed the kazoo to his mouth and blew one long monotone note. They perked up. He blew a second note, then a third, then burst into a rousing rendition of "Rudolph the Red Nose Reindeer." The toddlers applauded and jumped up and down to the unfamiliar melody.

Next he handed a kazoo to children, and then motioned for them to watch him as he hummed into his. They followed suit, spraying spit and slobber without song. Chuckling, he showed them again and again. They blew harder, their cheeks red, their eyes bulging. Pete laughed so hard he could barely manage repeat demonstrations.

Finally, MaiLy produced a sound from her kazoo. All eyes fixed on her and quiet fell over the group. She hummed into her instrument, again producing several shrilling notes. The others copied her technique until the room reverberated with sounds of joyful children blasting their musical scores.

Then MaiLy stepped away from the cacophonous crowd and gently hugged Pete's leg. He picked her up and she settled into his embrace.

"Merry Christmas," he whispered.

CHAPTER 8

Leaving MaiLy dimmed Pete's enthusiasm for going home. As the weeks before his departure droned by, ambivalent feelings wrestled inside him. He lay awake nights reliving moments he had spent with Mai, fantasizing about taking her home with him. In his foggy sleep he envisioned himself walking through the door of their home holding Mai. Connie would proudly place baby Marcie in his arms and he would put MaiLy in hers.

But that wasn't to be.

He had consulted with every attorney he could find in Saigon and Dalat. They all reiterated the problem of no agencies to facilitate adoptions. Connie had called every major adoption agency in the States and found the same disappointing answer.

"I'll find a way," he muttered half asleep. "Finding Mai was one of God's reasons for my coming here. I know she was created in His divine plan to be ours."

He punched his pillow a few times and rested his confused head on it. *And I'll miss my friends,* he thought. He had fallen in love with the country and its people and even dreamed of staying and sending for his family to join him. But the reality of the unpredictable war made that impossible.

He relived the day he was at his friend's home and helped deliver their baby. Covering his head with the sheet, he recalled helping them bury the infant six months later.

He had been invited to another friend's home to celebrate TET, the Vietnamese New Year; another honor bestowed him. Custom suggested that the virtues of the persons present in your home on this day are those that will bless your family for the coming year. Therefore, the Vietnamese selected only those guests with the finest traits to join them.

Pete rolled over another restless time recounting midnight mass in the cathedral as a guest of the Bishop. He had been one of a few Americans in the church, but felt a deep sense of community there.

Four days before he was to depart for the States he went to see Mai for the last time. She ran to him shouting, "Hi!" and jumped into his arms. He brought Tran along for this visit, hoping he could make Mai understand his feelings and his future plans for her.

After their usual photo sessions, foot-rides and kazoo harmonizing, he held her on his lap facing him. Her usual attempts to make him laugh had failed and the worried look on her face matched his.

"I am going away," Pete began. Mai shook her head at Tran when he interpreted the words.

"I have to. My work is done in Vietnam and I must go home to my family." She shook her head again and chattered a response to Tran.

"She's confused about the concept of family, Pete. She doesn't understand why you are leaving and asks if you will come back."

Pete choked back tears. "Maybe," he said. "If I can't come back I'll send someone to bring you to me."

Mai touched her chest, then his, and smiled as if she understood.

He carried her outside to the old rope swing. As they swayed he clutched her close. Her head rested on his shoulder.

"I love you, child of mine. I will not rest until you are with me. You have been the sunshine of my life this past year. Yet I know it was not meant to be for a year, but for a lifetime."

They swayed in silence for nearly an hour until he finally had to say, "Good-bye, my little girl."

Mai looked into his teary eyes and began to whimper.

He forced a smile until she did the same. He kissed her cheek, again committing the feeling to memory. She held his hand as they walked to the gate with the nun. Reaching down, he cupped her face in his hands, daring not to bend closer where she could see his tears. She threw her arms around his leg in the usual hug.

"I love you," was all he could say before walking through the gate and getting into the jeep.

He sobbed openly as Tran drove them down the hill and past the cemetery one last time.

CHAPTER 9

Pete's experience at the orphanage proved to be very helpful as he flaunted his diapering technique of six-month-old Marcie. The days at Fort Carson, Colorado were hectic, loving, and fun but not one passed that he did not think of MaiLy.

His replacement in Dalat had a Vietnamese wife and together they went to Domani de Marie periodically to check on MaiLy. Pete and Connie were pleased to read in their letters that she was doing well but distressed to read that she was being groomed to be a nun. Because of her intelligence and leadership, the nuns had plans to send her to a convent in France when she was older. So far Pete's efforts in the States had been futile for finding an adoption agency working in Vietnam.

He didn't know where to turn.

Six months later, in October of 1970, Pete was discharged from the army and moved his family to Denver. He was excited to finally put his law degree to work. Shortly after they settled in, he heard of an organization called Friends of Vietnam Children. *Bingo*, he thought, *this organization can help us get Mai.* He had been writing to her at the orphanage and prayed she would remember him until he found a way to get her out.

He and Connie went to an FVNC meeting the next month. The handful of volunteers raised food, medicine, and clothing for the Vietnam War orphans. Pete was all too aware of those needs and eagerly joined the group as a legal advisor. Connie coordinated a huge garage sale and within a year served on the board of directors. The organization confirmed the impossibility of Vietnamese adoptions but had plans to create those avenues soon.

Pete and Connie wrote to Sister Chantel of their rekindled hope to adopt MaiLy. No reply came. They wrote again and again. Many months passed before they received a letter that offered no hope.

They sent a letter to their friend, Cardinal Wright, and asked for a papal inquiry. A few months later, they received a letter from the Vatican. An emissary from Cardinal Wright had visited Domani de Marie.

Still no hope.

Then, in February 1973, after the Paris Peace Accords were signed and the American troops withdrawn, FVNC sent a delegation to Vietnam to negotiate a contract for adoptions there. Pete went as legal advisor, certain the trip was an answer to his years of prayer.

When the multitude of meetings was complete and the reams of paperwork signed, Pete set out for Dalat. A former Vietnamese associate in Saigon agreed to go along as his driver and interpreter. It had been three years since Pete had seen MaiLy. He couldn't allow his heart to hope she would remember him.

The beauty of the city and the fresh scent of pine provided a wonderful homecoming. Pete's heart danced to a familiar beat of happy anticipation, as the jeep approached Domani de Marie. He was encouraged to see Sister Chantel still there. Through the translator he recounted her agreement to let him adopt MaiLy if an agency was found to do so. Jubilantly, he told her he had just signed those very papers! Finally the process could begin to make Mai his daughter.

The nun frowned as she paced in front of him.

"Things have changed," she began. "She's not adoptable."

Pete's heart pounded so hard he could hardly hear her. "What do you mean?"

"I am told that MaiLy's mother is from a very wealthy, very strict Catholic family in Saigon. Because Mai was illegitimate, she could not keep her with her. She has signed her custody over to us, but may change her mind one day and want her back." Sister paced uncomfortably. "I am sorry, Mr. Mason. There is nothing I can do. Pick another child."

"I don't want another child!" Pete shouted. Then he forced himself to sit in the chair and take a deep breath. "There's part of this story you are not telling me."

Without speaking, the nun continued to pace. Finally she said in a pensive tone. "Perhaps I can talk with the Mother House and get them to sign a release to allow Mai to be adopted,"

"Oh, please," Pete begged. "I don't think even you believe this story about her mother. If your order has custody of her why won't they sign her release? Sister, you know how much I love her. You watched me with her for a year. You know we could give her a wonderful home."

Sister smiled her rare smile. "I'll see what I can do. I think I know how I can arrange it."

Suppressing his urge to kiss her, Pete began pumping her hand and stammering words of gratitude.

"Can I see her?"

Sister nodded then motioned for the younger nun to get MaiLy.

Pete sat fidgeting, wringing his sweaty hands. *She was only four when I left her,* he worried. *How can I expect her to remember me three years later?* He took out the photos of them together in hopes they would jog her memory.

When Pete saw Mai in the doorway standing shyly at the young nun's side, he stifled his urge to leap across the room and hug her. She was so much taller and so beautiful.

Mai's worried eyes searched the room as if looking for the reason she had been summoned to the office. When she spotted Pete, she jerked loose from the nun's hand and ran to him. He squatted to receive her embrace. She giggled as he stood and twirled her in his arms. She patted the tears from his cheeks, then placed hers against his. He eased back into the chair, with her still folded in his arms.

The nun resumed her pacing, then spoke one sentence to Mai.

Pete glared at his translator.

"Sister asked Mai if she wants to go away with you-- for you to be her father."

Pete froze as Mai sat silently on his lap. She seemed puzzled by the question.

The nun repeated it.

"Vang! Vang!" Mai nodded exuberantly.

"I think I can arrange the release," Sister said again.

Mai touched her chest, then Pete's, then pointed toward the door, with her head cocked to the side in question.

Pete shook his head. "Not today, Sweetie. But soon I'll be your daddy." He rocked her in his arms while his friend translated his words and sentiment to Mai.

"She must be really confused," Pete moaned. "I promised to come get her, but now I will leave again without her." They rocked together while Pete captured the moment in memory.

Then to lighten the mood he reached into his bag and pulled out his camera. Mai giggled, clapped her hands, and smiled into the lens. He snapped pose after pose. When he walked across the room, Mai sat on his foot, and laughed. This time her grip was above his knee. He pretended to struggle with his stride as he moved about the room until

48

they collapsed together in a hug. As she clenched her arms around his neck, he reveled in the sound of her laughter.

Too soon the younger nun returned and stood in the doorway. Pete understood the cue and stood to tell Mai good-bye-- again. As they pressed their cheeks together, he whispered, "I'll be back." Then to Sister Chantel he declared, "I'll be waiting for those release papers. I <u>will</u> be back and I will <u>never </u>leave here without her again."

His companion muttered the translation and the young nun extended her hand to MaiLy. After Sister Chantel's one word command, Mai patted Pete's cheek, stared into his red eyes, and jumped to the floor. Without looking back she took the nun's hand and walked away.

Pete returned to the States the next day.

Months passed.

Letters to Sister Chantel went unanswered and their usual donation checks uncashed.

Their fire of hope became a waning flicker. Only their relentless prayers gave breath to the dying flame. Each unanswered letter over the following year threatened to extinguish it.

The winter days skidded by until February, when Pete and Connie went to Vietnam to attend the 1975 International Conference on Child Welfare- -and to find and adopt MaiLy. After arriving in Saigon carrying dozens of boxes of supplies, they headed to the dock to help unload the rest they had shipped. After the 1973 trip, FVNC had set up a program in Saigon. Cherie Clark, a homemaker and volunteer from Illinois, became the overseas director. Cherie and her husband had moved their four birth children to Saigon and had since adopted five Vietnamese children.

Pete helped unload the ton of supplies, including a washing machine and an Isolette for the dozen babies in their intensive care nursery.

The conference was intriguing but as soon as it was over, he and Connie headed for Domani de Marie. With them they took Thuy, a social worker for FVNC who had attended the University of Minnesota.

"Sister Chantel isn't here, now," Thuy said, translating the Mother Superior's statement.

"Here we go again," Pete muttered to Connie with gritted teeth. She took his hand, knowing it would calm him.

Patiently, Pete began to speak and Thuy echoed his historic account of his relationship with Mai and the promises made by Sister Chantel. This nun had no knowledge of the many letters they had written over the past five years, but seemed genuinely moved by their frustrating story.

Mai's housemother entered and introduced herself as Sister Katrine. As she talked on about how well Mai was doing, her own love for the child shone through.

"Please, may we see her?" Pete finally asked.

"I'll tell her she has a visitor." Sister Katrine smiled. Pete sat on the edge of his chair squeezing Connie's hand.

"It's been two more years," he moaned. "I can't expect her to remember me this time."

"Show her the pictures you brought," Connie said, putting her arm around him. "With Thuy's help, she'll remember you."

Pete stood when he heard the trampling of small feet getting faster and faster in the hall. The door burst open and MaiLy ran through it and jumped into his arms. He fell back into the chair and cried while Connie hugged them both.

Sister Katrine pulled a kerchief from her sleeve and wiped her eyes.

Mai kept her arms wrapped around Pete's neck as she rubbed her cheek against his. Then everyone's tears were erased by giggles as Mai sat bouncing on his knee. When Connie reached for Mai, she nestled even closer into Pete's embrace.

"We don't see many red-heads around here," Thuy explained and even the nuns laughed.

"Mai, this is Connie," Pete said as he put his arm around his wife. Mai smiled weakly with her head on Pete's shoulder.

Mother Superior shuffled papers and stared down at her desk while she repeated the story of Mai's mother being alive. When Pete quizzed her, she simply shook her head, refusing to give details. He grilled her for more information. Finally she admitted that the mother had signed relinquishment papers so Domani de Marie had custody of MaiLy.

Pete heaved a sigh of relief.

Thuy translated the next hurdle. MaiLy would be adoptable only if the Mother House in Saigon would sign the appropriate papers.

"After what I've seen here today, I don't think that will be a problem," the nun concluded. "I'll write and recommend it immediately."

Connie and Pete hugged with Mai between them.

Plans were made for Mai to accompany them on an outing the next day. Thuy explained the plan to Mai and this time she left the room cheerfully.

Thuy rode into Dalat with the driver but Pete and Connie opted to walk. As they strolled hand in hand past the orchid fields and vegetable plantations, they talked of their renewed hope of adopting Mai.

"If she has a mother she should be with her," Pete said. "But it breaks my heart to see her living year after year without a family."

"So we'll be her family," Connie said.

CHAPTER 10

Saigon, Vietnam, April 5, 1975

The tranquil golden sunrise offered even greater hope as the raft of refugees drifted toward the coast and the Saigon skyline came into view. The men shook hands and slapped each other's backs and the women laughed and hugged the children. As they neared the beach, they were greeted by the familiar sounds of a city in panic. The tide washed their craft to the shore where those with similar dreams had abandoned similar rafts. Mai's legs crumpled beneath her as she stepped off the raft and onto the sand. The travelers supported one other as they joined the thousands of fleeing refugees mobbing the landing docks.

Sister Katrine and Mai followed the group on their trek to the United States embassy. They snaked a path through throngs of screaming people pushing their way to the docks. Thousands on carts, scooters, and foot pressed their way to freedom. Some ran with mattresses over their heads in case the distant explosions came near.

Sister and her companions stopped to buy food from vendors trying to raise money for their own escape, bargaining to purchase it at a reasonable price. They picked fruit from trees and sat amidst the clamor to feed their bodies and their perseverance. Mai ate ferociously allowing the juices to drip onto her chin and clothes. She smiled, longing for the box of cookies the redheaded lady had bought her at the end of their outing together a few months ago. Mai had hidden them in her room and eaten them slowly, savoring them, until the nuns discovered the near-empty box. They had punished Mai by making her spend the night in the chicken coop.

It was midday before their group arrived at the gates of the U.S. Embassy. Armed guards kept hundreds at bay, allowing only a few through at a time. Those waiting waved papers and promises while screaming their pleas for admission.

"Come with us," the young woman pleaded to Sister Katrine, then turned to her husband.

"Perhaps we can help you escape with us," he offered.

"No, but thank you for all you have already done for us," Sister said, extending her hand. "I must find the organization that wants to take Mai to a family waiting in America. I cannot remember the name," she added, shaking her head in disgust. "So I will go to our Mother House here. Perhaps they can help me."

She bade them good-bye, then summoned a two-wheeled taxi to weave MaiLy and her through the screeching, honking horde of panicking civilians. Mai dozed fitfully beside her as the taxi was pulled through the legion of refugees. Hours later it jerked to a halt. Sister Katrine sighed a smile when she read Sisters of Charity of St. Vincent de Paul on a building sign. She helped Mai to the ground and paid the driver from her dwindling fund. When he told her of his efforts to raise money for his family's escape, she pressed an extra coin into his palm.

Inside, the nuns welcomed them with a big meal, warm baths, and beds. Mai refused to lie down and pouted until she was permitted to play with the other children in the shaded courtyard. When she noticed MaiLy already playing with a little girl in a wheelchair, Sister Katrine admitted she felt ill. After a nap she would share her story and purpose for being there.

As Sister Katrine rested, Mother Superior opened the door for the two visitors.

"I am Thuy," the Vietnamese woman said. "This is Cherie Clark, director of Friends of Vietnam Children here in Saigon. Her agency has done much to help our children." Mother Superior gestured for them to enter but did not suggest they be seated. "The United States has organized a giant airlift to help take orphans from our country before we are soon defeated." The nun frowned. Thuy went on. "We are here to offer help if you want us to assist in getting your children to America."

"We can take care of our own children," the nun scowled.

Thuy bowed slightly. "Certainly, in normal circumstances you do, Mother Superior. But the war is threatening our city now and there is much fear that the children will suffer. Many of the children you care for are crippled or are of mixed race. There are terrible predictions of what will happen to them if the Communists take over."

The nun didn't speak but stood firm. Cherie wrote on a piece of paper and asked Thuy to tell the nun to contact them if she changed her mind. The nun placed the paper in the desk drawer and started to lead them to the door. Cherie chattered a message for Thuy to translate.

"We have a second purpose in coming here today," Thuy said quickly. She and Cherie stood still. "We have been to your orphanage in Dalat and have a deep concern for its welfare since it fell to the Communists a few days ago." The nun looked surprised.

"Ask her if she knows what happened to the children there, especially Mai," Cherie coaxed. Thuy translated the question but the nun just shook her head. Thuy walked about the room to buy time and gently repeated the question. The nun didn't respond.

Thuy gazed out the window into the courtyard and watched the children at play. The nun walked toward the door again, in an obvious attempt to escort them out.

"Cherie, there's Mai!" Thuy gasped. Then she hollered, "There's Mai!" Cherie looked where Mai played with a child on crutches. Knocking on the window, Thuy called her name. The nun opened the door to the courtyard, a perplexed look on her face. Cherie and Thuy ran toward Mai, but then slowed their pace so they wouldn't frighten her.

"Are all the children from Domani de Marie here?" Thuy asked. The nun shrugged.

"This little girl has been promised to a family in America," Cherie said. The nun seemed even more suspicious when Thuy translated that claim.

"I have no authority to release this child," the nun said flatly.

"Please," Cherie begged, then noticed Thuy muttering into Mai's ear.

"Take to America," Cherie stammered in an attempt to stall.

The nun shook her head. Thuy continued to talk to Mai in a low tone. When she finished, Mai nodded. To the nun Thuy said, "A family in America is waiting to adopt this child who they have loved for seven years. Please look into this and you will find it is so."

"If what you say is true, I will bring this child to you tomorrow morning," the nun promised hesitantly.

"Thank you, Sister, thank you," Cherie said shaking her hand. The three walked back inside the building while Thuy explained Mai's story and the Masons' love for her.

Thuy and Cherie turned to wave to Mai who stood looking lost and confused.

As they descended the orphanage steps, Cherie asked Thuy what she whispered to Mai.

"I'm not sure the nun believes us, so I'm not at all sure she will bring her to us tomorrow. Besides, I'm not certain that Sister Chantel even got the release papers she promised Pete in January. So I told Mai that we wanted to take her to the Masons. I told her that when she leaves mass tomorrow noon, turn left to the corner, not right with the group. I promised we would be there to take her away."

CHAPTER 11

Cherie looked out the doorway of the FVNC Center and watched a dilapidated car make its way up the driveway. She watched as two nuns stepped out of the car.

"I can't believe she's here," Cherie whispered to herself, then shouted, "Thuy, she's here!"

Slowly, Mai exited the car and stood hiding behind the nun's long black habit. Cherie and Thuy walked to Mai, then bent to welcome her. MaiLy shook her head and stepped farther behind the nun.

"We'll wait inside," Cherie said sympathetically.

Sister Katrine squatted to Mai's level. "Do you remember the special man who came to visit you at the orphanage many times?" Mai nodded. "He lives far away. If I leave you here they will take you to him."

"But I don't want you to leave me," Mai whimpered, stepping closer to her.

"I cannot go, MaiLy. I must stay and care for other children."

"But you always care for me," Mai reminded her.

"Now someone else will care for you, MaiLy. You will have a family."

"But I don't want you to go away," Mai said, resting her head on Sister's shoulder. "You are my family."

Sister took a handkerchief from her sleeve and wiped her eyes. "Haven't I always taken good care of you MaiLy?" Mai nodded.

"Now I can take the best care of you by letting you go." Mai wrapped her arms around Sister Katrine's neck.

"Remember, God will take care of you-- and will give you beautiful rainbows after storms," Sister whispered.

Then she took Mai's hand and led her to the steps.

Mai stood crying and waving goodbye to the only family she'd ever known.

Cherie led Mai inside where dozens of babies lay on mats covering the floor. Thuy explained that these were babies like those at Domani de Marie and they were all gathered here to get ready to leave for America, like Mai. The sound of crying infants provided Mai with that strange sense of familiar belonging again. She sat next to one, picked it up, and rocked it in her arms. Thuy and Cherie exchanged smiles and resumed the frantic task of airlift preparations.

Nearly 100 babies blanketed the floor of the two-story building. Cribs lined the walls and mats covered the tiled floors. On every mat there were several babies sleeping, crying, and cooing. Some were beautifully healthy. Others were deformed or sickly. Nursery smells of wet dirty diapers, vomit, baby powder, and formula were multiplied tenfold in the hot, humid building.

The infants had all been brought from the FVNC foster homes. A measles outbreak, a few years before, taught a fatal lesson on the problem of having all the children in one facility. Ads were placed in newspapers recruiting breast-feeding woman to care for orphaned babies in their homes.

Breast milk provided the perfect nutrition and disease-resisting antibodies. Equally important was the cuddling the foster mothers gave the infants. A physician and social worker visited them on a weekly basis providing supplies and assistance.

Now the babies were gathered again in babbling harmony.

Many of the foster mothers joined the dozen Vietnamese workers in colorful smocks, lovingly tending the scores of fussing babies. Smells of dirty diapers and spit-up permeated the humid air.

An American woman sat next to Mai and smiled. Mai smiled back, faintly, while cooing to the baby she was holding.

Eventually the woman coaxed Mai to follow her to the kitchen area where older children and toddlers were eating. Mai refused to join them and sat alone picking at her food. She pictured herself eating at Domani de Marie with Minh and her other friends. She squinted hard to keep from crying when she realized that she was never going to know those surroundings again.

As night fell she was directed to a mat on the floor next to several other girls and boys her age. She never imagined she would long for her drab room and the gray blanket on the cot at the orphanage. Wrapping her arms around herself, she tried not to cry as she listened to the crying babies and drifted to sleep.

Mai woke to the sound of one hundred babies at the FVNC Center, all awake pleading for breakfast. She rubbed her red, puffy eyes and stared at her surroundings. As usual, to ease her sorrow, she began daydreaming - - this time about her school days at Domani de Marie.

"MaiLy!" She could almost hear the teacher's curt voice as she recalled sitting in a trance at her wooden school desk.

"Let me count your pages next," Father had called.

Mai carried her notebook to the desk in front of the class. The priest leafed through the pages, counting them one at a time. Mai knew that even one missing page would result in punishment. She hoped he wouldn't notice the page she had torn out and used to catch a bug. The ruler's wallop on her hand told her he had noticed, all right. Mai stifled a yelp and returned to her seat. She looked at Minh, sitting near her with a look of sympathy on her face. Mai set her chin firmly and swallowed the tears choking in her throat.

Mercifully, the bell clanged, calling for recess. The parade of six-year-olds, all in blue uniforms, marched quietly out of the classroom. The orphanage playground was more like a barren, dusty lot. The children had to find their own fun, like digging for bugs in the dirt. Mai knew she wouldn't misuse a blank page from her notebook again, no matter how entertaining the bug promised to be.

Mihn re-traced the hopscotch pattern in the soft earth and took the first turn jumping through the squares. Mai took her turn with such comical speed; she plopped to the ground making everyone giggle. The three other girls copied her antics until they were all coughing and laughing in a cloud of dust.

Too soon, Father rang the gold hand bell again. The girls stood, brushing the dirt from their blue plaid jumpers and elbows of their white blouses. They knew this mess would result in another scolding.

Silently, the youngsters filed into the classroom. The gray bare walls reflected Mai's mood. She slumped into the black wrought iron seat attached to her small wooden desk. Obediently, she dipped her pen in the corner ink hole and began her penmanship assignment.

Next, she tried to pay attention as the instructor's chalk grated across the old blackboard forming math problems. She copied them down on her paper accurately, and then double-checked her numbers. Last time she had written them hastily and incorrectly and was made to stand in front of the class with her arms extended, a rock in each hand.

Though it seemed like hours passed, Minh had estimated it to be only a ten-minute punishment.

Mai was sad and angry when reprimanded for small infractions. She wasn't angry with the priest or nuns, but with herself for having misbehaved. In spite of their strict discipline, Mai knew they cared about her. Especially Sister Katrine. She always seemed to have a special smile for Mai or a gentle pat when no one was looking.

The bell rang again and the children walked out of the room with great restraint, then broke into a run when they reached the door. They raced to their cottages, changed into their colored tunic shirts and matching pants, and headed to the fields for an hour's work before supper. Income from raising artichokes, cabbages, tomatoes, and strawberries provided the major support for Domani de Marie Orphanage and the nuns relied heavily on the work of the children to maintain the crops. The youngsters were taught a sense of pride and ownership by contributing to their own welfare.

Mai kicked off her sandals, as usual, and ran barefoot to the field. There were not enough straw hats for each child, but today she was lucky to wear one. She appreciated it not only because it blocked the sun from her face, but also because it blocked Sister's view of her munching an occasional forbidden strawberry. Mai had it down to an art. She bit into the three-inch fruit while inhaling, so no juice dripped down her shirt to tattle on her. She was grateful for these short after-school work sessions and dreaded Saturday's full day of fieldwork.

When the supper bell rang, she raced Minh back to their cottage. Even barefoot, Mai always won. She no longer felt the stones beneath her callused feet. She knew the bell rang only once, and anyone who was not at the table for grace, missed the meal.

Another lesson Mai had learned the hard way.

She and Minh splashed cold water from the pump on their hands and faces and each other as they washed. Giggling, they ran to supper. It was always the same - - bits of meat mixed with rice, and plenty of fruits and vegetables. Every plate had to be clean before the group was dismissed and second helpings were rare. The children cleared the tables, which then became study areas. After completing their arithmetic problems, Mai and her ten classmates began the daily memorization of other lessons. The nuns were very strict about each being recited precisely as written in the book.

Back at the cottage, Mai sat on the edge of her bed after finishing the daily task of washing her own uniform. She stared at the two other cots, each covered by a gray blanket. The room was as colorless and desolate as her life. When the curtains separating the beds were pulled, she changed into her nightclothes. She knelt beside her bed in the proper posture for prayer - - back straight, hands perfectly folded with fingertips pointing up. She recited all the prayers she could remember. Then she crawled into bed and buried her face in her pillow so her roommates wouldn't hear her cry - - again.

Every night she prayed.

Every night she cried.

And yearned for the man that promised to come for her.

The boy sleeping next to her began thrashing in his sleep and Mai's daydream was interrupted. The scores of babbling babies, toddlers, and FVNC workers finally woke him too. He smiled so Mai smiled back. He called himself Michael, which Mai thought was a strange name. Taking her hand, he led her to the kitchen where a dozen youngsters sat around a long table, laughing and gobbling their food. Her new friend's smile was infectious and she soon found herself joining in the breakfast commotion. She watched as youngsters bounced in their chairs and grabbed food with their hands. With a sly smile she hesitantly joined in the ill-mannered meal. Before long, her pig imitation over the cooked gruel won her the admiration and friendship of all those present. The adults seemed too busy and preoccupied to notice, so her raucous encore was well received. She half expected to feel the tap of Sister Katrine's hand on her head and felt sadder than relieved when she didn't.

A shady verandah provided a place for Mai to teach her new playmates the game of hopscotch. A girl about Mai's age with light brown hair and skin sat silently on a bench, her face completely without expression. She wore a white straw hat with part of the brim folded back. Mai postponed her play to listen to the Vietnamese workers whisper her story. The child's mother had carried her from Danang to Saigon. The mother told the nuns the girl had witnessed the slaughter of half-white children when the Communists took over Danang. Because she was Amerasian, the mother feared for her daughter's life. She had pulled the wide-brimmed hat over the child's face and carried her over 300 miles to the orphanage for protection.

"No wonder she sits with such a blank look on her face," another worker commented. "She has seen a bit of hell."

Mai shivered as she recalled running through bombing outside the orphanage gate and seeing one soldier blast open the chest of another.

"That's why Sister Katrine let me go," she muttered to herself. "To save my life." Gratitude and love slowly dimmed her sadness. "Maybe they are telling me the truth here. Maybe they are taking me to the man who promised to come back for me."

She ambled to a less crowded area on the verandah and sat in the shade of a tree to enjoy one of her favorite memories - - her last day with him.

Her eyes had widened as Sister Katrine opened the big gift box and unfolded a yellow dress and red sweater he had sent. Mai held it to her shoulders and twirled. Minh and her other friends squealed and clapped then helped her put it on. They took turns stroking the crisp cotton fabric. Next Sister unwrapped a new pair of sandals and the girls oohed and ahhed. Reverently, Mai buckled them on her feet and skipped around the room.

Sister explained that the gifts were from the Masons who had visited Mai the day before. They would return and take her on an outing today. Mai danced and spun and hugged her friends. Sister settled them down and talked at length about proper behavior for a young lady.

The rest of the box was filled with supplies and gifts for the other children. Soon Pete arrived with Connie and Mai gave him her usual greeting. After touring the orphanage complex with the nuns, they all headed to the gate where Thuy waited with the car. Mai skipped along at Pete's side and exited the gate without hesitation.

As they strolled the beautiful streets of Dalat, the red headed woman continuously snapped pictures of Mai and tried to hold her hand. Confused by all this attention, and the woman's constant stares and hand gestures, Mai turned to Thuy for an explanation. When told the woman wanted to be her mother, Mai felt confused but admitted this was the happiest she had ever felt.

They entered an exquisite hotel and were seated at a table dressed with fine linen, cut glass, and pewter. Mai gawked around trying to take in the fantasy-like surroundings. A part of her, though, wished she were back at the orphanage in a more familiar setting. She recalled the lecture Sister Katrine had given her and tried to sit like a grown-up.

Pete placed a bubbly brown drink in front of her. Until now, her only beverage had been lukewarm milk. She watched Pete pick up his glass and sip from the straw. Mai held hers and did likewise.

She swallowed, then giggled.

She swallowed again and giggled louder.

By the third sip she was laughing out loud, as were Connie, Pete, and Thuy. Mai guzzled the drink, and said, "Them nua!"

Thuy told Pete Mai wanted more cola and he summoned the waiter to oblige. Mai consumed the refill without stopping for breath. "Them nua!"

When Pete suggested she wait awhile, she gave him a look that would have really disappointed Sister Katrine.

The next entree was ice cream mounded high in a pewter dish. Mai touched the pewter bowl and jerked her hand away. Everyone laughed. Pete dipped his spoon into his serving and placed it in his mouth. Mai heaped a portion on her spoon, then bulged her cheeks as she started to chew. The look of discomfort and fear melted into one of pleasure as she swallowed the dessert.

She gobbled hers down before the others were finished and her demand for more went unanswered, even with the pouting face she reconstructed. Pete took her to the window seat and placed her on the cushion. She didn't understand his words but his voice and gestures reminded her of how much he loved her. The feelings swelling in her heart were unlike any she had ever felt.

They walked in the market place and the redheaded lady held Pete's hand. MaiLy pulled away whenever she tried to hold hers. When Mai pointed to any item, she bought it - - even a white hat with flowers and a bird on the brim. They all sat together on a bench and Thuy told Mai how much the American couple loved her. She expounded on what a wonderful person Mai was; compliments she had never heard before.

When the sun settled on the horizon, they returned to the orphanage. Thuy tried to explain but Mai couldn't understand her fate. Thuy repeated how this couple wanted to be her mother and father - - that they wanted to take her away from here but could not today.

Mai only had to look into Pete's eyes to know that he was leaving her again. This day that had held her greatest joy now held her greatest sadness.

She whimpered and clung to Pete's neck. Connie cried as she hugged her good-bye, and gave her a package of cookies.

Sister Katrine took Mai's hand and began leading her away. Mai broke loose of her hold and ran back to where Pete squatted with open arms.

She didn't understand his words, but his eyes told her he was coming back.

CHAPTER 12

Denver, Colorado, April 5, 1975

Pete bolted out of bed when the telephone rang at three a.m. But Connie had beaten him to the hall phone. He could hear her crying.

"It's Leah, from Georgia FVNC. A ham radio operator there heard that a planeload of orphans crashed in Saigon."

They held each other and cried for an hour, wondering how such a catastrophe could happen and how they would cope if it had.

"We were just there a few months ago," Connie mumbled. "I can't bear to think about the babies and our staff …"

"Let's try to call Cherie in Saigon," Pete suggested.

"We cannot place a call to Saigon at this time," the operator said. "However, we'll be happy to book you a phone call in July."

"July! July! There may not be a South Vietnam in July!" Pete slammed the receiver. "I'm calling my buddy, Bernie, in the State Department." Pete and Bernie had served together in Vietnam. If anyone could tell them the truth, Bernie could.

"Vietnam desk. Bernie Salvo."

Pete told his friend what he had heard. "Tell me it isn't true."

"There's information coming in on the crash, Pete, but we haven't been able to confirm who it was. That's why I haven't called you."

"Ask him where FVNC's place was on the board, " Connie whispered. "They post all flights planned in and out of Vietnam."

"Who was listed on the board as the next expected flight out, Bernie?"

"FVNC."

"Oh, no! Please, God, no!"

"We don't know anything for sure, Pete. Let me keep on this and I'll call you as soon as I confirm things."

With robot-like motion, Connie and Pete dressed, took her daughters to school, and then went together to the FVNC headquarters to wait for Bernie's call. News of President Ford's Operation Babylift had hit the press two days ago, so Pete and Connie weren't surprised to find reporters outside the office. They hustled past the cameras and pretended to smile as they answered questions about the anticipated airlift. Inside they found little refuge. The phone rang non-stop all morning. The mailman, who normally toted a shoulder pack, arrived in a truck to deliver huge bags of mail from supportive citizens and prospective families.

When they couldn't get a line for outgoing calls, they decided to go home to continue business. Reporters from Associated Press greeted them there, hammering them with questions about a rumored plane crash of orphans.

"Nothing is confirmed," Pete and Connie repeated as they maneuvered their way into their home. There, the unceasing phone calls dominated their day, battering their patience and assaulting their hopes.

Another three a.m. phone call jolted them from bed. They both raced to the hall phone, stumbling and bumping into walls. Connie yanked the phone to her ear.

"Connie, this is Cherie in Saigon." At first her voice was clear, then it began to fade. "It wasn't us!"

"What?" Connie had to hear this message right.

"It wasn't us!" Cherie shouted again. The tidal wave of joy receded when Cherie said, "It was another agency. Hundreds of babies and volunteers died." Connie could hear Cherie's tears. "It was supposed to be us, but we were bumped from first place yesterday."

The signal was getting much weaker. Connie thought she heard Cherie chuckling.

"We've got Mai!"

"What?"

"We've got Mai!" Cherie yelled again with a fading laugh

"You've got Mai?"

Pete's haggard face lit up.

"It's not our plane!" Connie told him. "And she's got MaiLy!" The line went dead. Connie dropped the phone and twirled in her husband's arms as they cried and took turns repeating, "They've got our Mai!"

CHAPTER 13

"MaiLy." It was Michael calling her to lunch. They tiptoed through the sea of babbling babies at the FVNC Center. Ross, a young American with brown hair and a bushy mustache, joined them at the long wooden table. His silly magic tricks and teasing brought much needed laughter to Mai and her new friends.

After lunch they remained in the dining area to draw and color with crayons and paper Ross provided. A short time later he came bounding back into the room. "It is time! Our first plane to America is about to leave!"

Some of Mai's playmates clapped and danced about. Others looked as confused as Mai felt. Dozens of workers began to dress the scores of babies in nice clothes, many of them weeping as they did. Mai touched the hand of one tearful worker and asked why she was crying.

"The babies are leaving us," the woman in the smock said.

"Don't you want them to go?" Mai asked while helping to stuff the wiggling arm into a sleeper.

70

"Oh, yes," the worker replied quickly. "But I have cared for this baby in my home for nearly a year. I cry that he will be happy in America, but I will miss him very much."

Mai walked to the kitchen where workers were preparing hundreds of bottles of formula. The American woman, LeAnn, was there and smiled broadly at Mai as she cautioned the workers against boiling the milk in the bottles. A worker smiled as she explained the plan was deliberate. The formula would cool to the perfect temperature by the time the babies needed it on the plane.

All the babies were awake now and most of them crying as they were being dressed, then carried to a van waiting outside. From there they were taken to a huge city bus at the end of the narrow street. The adults were nearly running to the van with a baby in each arm, and yelling to be heard above the noise of fussing children. Cherie stopped calling out orders long enough to stoop and hug Mai. MaiLy stood stiffly, still not understanding why this woman seemed to care for her so.

Michael appeared at her side. He quickly answered her questions about what was going on.

"The war is coming soon. Have you seen the soldiers and the guns and heard the bombing far away?"

Mai nodded

"We must leave quick before the bombs kill us like they did my mother and father." He wiped his eyes. "No one knows how many plane loads will be allowed to leave. That is why they must get as many babies and children on as possible - - and fast."

Together they walked to the van and watched as LeAnn placed squalling babies around her on the bench seat. Then Ross put twenty more at her feet on the floor of the van.

Mai and Michael put their hands over their ears, shook their heads and giggled as the babies kept crying. They watched as the van left and returned several times to load more infants.

Cherie came to give Mai another hug, then motioned her inside the van. MaiLy gripped Michael's hand and pulled him along. Cherie smiled, nodded, and helped them both in. She kissed Mai's cheek and tousled Michael's hair before other children crowded around them. Soon the van door slammed shut and they crept through the side street to the waiting city bus. There, Mai was directed to get on and sit in a backbench seat. Two fussing babies were placed on each side of her. A Vietnamese worker instructed her to watch the babies so they didn't roll when the bus began to move. Mai patted the back of the baby on her left and stroked the cheek of the one on her right, but they continued to cry. The sound of dozens of crying babies reverberated off the sides of the metal bus, which was becoming more like an oven in the 104 degree heat. The little ones flailed their hands and legs while their tears and sweat pooled on the plastic seats beside them. Ross and the American volunteers frantically danced from seat to seat comforting as many babies as possible. The formula, still scalding hot, could offer no relief to the dehydrating, squalling infants.

Mercifully, the bus inched forward, slithering through the over-crowded streets to Tan Son Nhut Airport. The motion rocked the babies and the crying lessened.

Mai wiped the sweat from her own face and sang softly to the babies still whimpering at her side. They didn't seem to mind that Mai only knew church hymns.

She patted and sang and wondered if she would ever see or hear the babies from Domani de Marie again.

After nearly an hour, the bus pulled along side a huge airplane and stopped. The crying increased as workers from the Center helped loaded them one by one onto the waiting C-5A cargo jet.

When the last baby had been carried off, Mai sat alone in the back of the bus, not understanding what was happening or what she was to do next.

She felt as empty and hollow as the abandoned bus.

Ross bounded up the steps in one jump, and slowly walked back to MaiLy. He pushed his glasses back on his sweaty face and squatted in the aisle beside her. She didn't understand his words, but the kindness in his eyes told her to take his extended hand. He led her off the bus to the steps of the plane. Mai halted and jerked her hand away.

Airplanes meant bombing and destruction.

Ross looked at her knowingly, lifted her into his strong arms, and they boarded together.

All the seats had been removed from the center of the plane; only bench seats remained on the sides. Mai grinned when she saw Michael there. Ross gently placed Mai beside her friend, patted her leg, and turned his attention to the 100 babies in open cardboard boxes.

Twenty, two-foot-square cartons had been placed in a row down the middle of the gutted plane. Two or three babies lay in each box. A long strap extended over the line of boxes and attached to the other end of the plane, securing the makeshift cribs in place. Several metal trash cans sat at each end, filled with formula, diapers and supplies for the journey.

The nine adults on board nervously took their seats and the plane engine whirled. Michael fidgeted in his seat and seemed as worried as the others.

"Two days ago a plane like this, with babies and grown-ups, crashed after it took-off," Michael said. Mai thought she hadn't heard him correctly above the roar of the plane engine as it began its taxi down the runway. When he repeated the statement, the message was the same. No one knew if the plane had been shot down or sabotaged. Half of the 250 orphans and many of the adults had died.

Mai gripped Michael's trembling hand and huddled closer to him as she felt the plane lift off the runway. There was an eerie silence that even the babies seemed to respect as the plane began its ascent. The adults stared at one another with looks of anguish on their faces.

The plane shook and everyone gasped in unison, but then the ride smoothed again. Mai gawked out the window with terror racing through her heart. Tears stung her eyes as she watched the land grow more distant.

The pilot made an announcement and everyone clapped and heaved sighs of relief.

"We are safe now," Michael hollered. "No bombs can reach us here!" Mai tried to return his comforting look, but her heart was still pounding with fright.

The nine adults unbuckled their seat belts and merrily began the work of feeding and diapering one hundred bawling babies. Mai swallowed her fear and jumped from her seat on the sidelines. She pulled on Ross's pant leg and extended her open arms. Ross sat her beside him, placed a baby in her lap, and handed Mai a bottle. He sat beside her and demonstrated the feeding technique with the baby she was holding. Mai followed his unspoken instructions and the baby in her arms gulped the formula, which seemed to be the perfect temperature. Mai giggled and so did Ross as he nodded his approval.

Volunteers fed several babies at a time by placing them on their sides in the boxes and propping their bottles on the shoulder of their box-mate. As bottles emptied, the workers held babies to burp them. With diapers draping their shoulders, they could burp one baby with one hand while feeding a second with the other.

Some babies suckled formula down in only minutes while others needed more help. LeAnn cradled a baby girl in her folded legs and coaxed her to drink. The baby, too weak to cry or suckle, allowed the nipple to fall from her lips. LeAnn milked the formula from the bottle into the baby's mouth and she swallowed it one drop at a time.

Soon the plane was filled with the smell of diarrhea and spit-up, but no one seemed to mind. The adults and older children worked happily for hours until the pilot announced a fuel stop in the Philippines.

Mai was buckled into her bench seat again as the plane descended and bumped onto the runway. She gazed out the window at the palm trees and smiled with relief when she saw the sandy brown earth. She nudged Michael. "Vietnam!" she beamed.

"No," said Michael soberly. "We will never see Vietnam again."

Mai pressed her face against the window. Her tears trickled down the glass.

CHAPTER 14

Babies gently bumped against each other as the plane came to a halt. Dozens of American women waited on the landing strip, then entered the plane one at a time to carry infants to the waiting buses.

"We're military wives here at Clark Air Force Base," one pretty blonde explained to LeAnn.

"I thought we were just stopping for fuel. Why are the babies being loaded onto buses?" LeAnn asked, cuddling the infant in her arms.

"No, you'll be here for at least one day so the babies can have medical check-ups and better plane accommodations can be made."

Mai watched nervously as the parade of women entered one end of the plane, and exited the other with a baby. A chubby lady with brown hair and a big smile crouched in front of Mai and spoke softly. Her gestures suggested Mai accompany her off the plane. Reluctantly, Mai took her hand and followed her down the stairs, across the sun-baked tarmac, and onto an open-air bus. As they left the airstrip, a cool breeze blew Mai's hair from her face. She leaned her worried head against the window and gazed solemnly at the scenery. These palm trees seemed to wave a tranquility unknown in Vietnam. The orderly streets carried only two lanes of traffic.

There was no congestion of carts, bicycles, and oxen.

No thunderous bombings.

No hordes of frightened people.

No Domani de Marie.

No Sister Katrine.

The chubby lady took a handkerchief and wiped the tears from Mai's face, then gently patted her hand.

The bus stopped in front of a gigantic building where even more America women greeted the children. They were escorted inside to find hundreds of mattresses in neat rows on the gymnasium floor. Each mattress had a stack of baby supplies at the end and a volunteer to care for each child.

A lady sitting on the end of her assigned mattress welcomed Mai. The woman extended her arms but Mai avoided her embrace and lay on the clean sheets, hugging herself. The woman covered her with a blanket and stroked her head until Mai fell asleep.

Mai spent most of the next two days curled up on her mattress. Every eight hours a new, smiling woman took a shift as her caregiver. Mai obeyed their gestures to eat, bathe, and sleep, but avoided their attempts to read to her or involve her with other children. Hundreds more babies, toddlers, and older children filled the gym. Laughter and chatter echoed throughout the sunny building, but Mai remained despondent.

Again and again she asked where she was going. But no one understood. No one answered. Finally a Vietnamese interpreter was summoned to respond to her question. The answer "America" was meaningless to Mai.

When the interpreter insisted she join the other children in games, Mai resumed her fetal position.

Early the third morning, volunteers loaded babies and children back onto buses and took them to the airport. There a mammoth plane waited. It wasn't green and brown like others Mai had seen. This one shone silver in the dawn sunlight. Maybe that's why she wasn't afraid to board this time.

Most of the seats inside the DC-10 had a cardboard box strapped in them. Volunteers entered the back of the plane with a baby in their arms, placed it in a box, and exited near the cabin. The parade continued until the aircraft reverberated with the sounds of 300 anxious babies. Eighty escorts took their places next to the four children in their charge. As the plane taxied down the runway, a flight attendant spoke by microphone from the front of the plane orienting the volunteers to the layout of the facilities, the use of oxygen masks, and the location of infant supplies.

Mai stared blankly, straight ahead, as her escort tried unsuccessfully to play a game with the children he was tending. Her companions, all near her age, resisted his efforts to make them smile. Mai's stoic state ended when she heard the young girl beside her stifling sobs. Mai scooted closer to her and quietly placed her arm around the girl's shoulder. The youngster rested her head against Mai's and wept out loud. The man looked on, his eyes moist, as he watched Mai join in tears of consolation.

The eight-hour flight to Hawaii went quickly. While escorts busily changed diaper after diaper and fed baby after baby, an Associated Press reporter sat typing frantically.

Helpers congested the aisles as they fetched supplies and feedings for the children in their care. One volunteer rocked a baby with skinny legs in one arm while bottle-feeding a baby with a bloated belly in the other. Toddlers clung to their caregivers, seemingly begging for affection. Laughter and chatter provided a constant concert, and Mai slowly joined in the tune.

The pilot announced a stop in Hawaii to refuel. The volunteers groaned in unison when he added all passengers must deplane during fueling.

When the aircraft came to a complete halt, the older children and adults jumped to their feet to leave. They slumped back into their seats when they were told volunteers would enter one at a time and exit with a child as before.

The process took nearly two hours, while those babies still waiting vocalized their protests. When Mai and her new friends began racing in the aisles, they were allowed to leave next.

They could hardly believe the site that greeted them inside. Hundreds of babies, toddlers, and volunteers packed every inch of the terminal. Clowns, balloons, and tables of food welcomed the older children. Mai had never seen a clown before, but when the others laughed at his comical antics, she joined in the fun. She pulled scarves out of his sleeve as directed by his gestures. Her smile widened with each continuous link of scarf and she laughed when the final one topped the pile on the floor.

She and her friends followed their escorts to the food tables. No one seemed concerned with the quantity or neatness of the food consumed, so Mai dug in with bare hands and ate ravenously.

By now the entire terminal was so jammed with people it was nearly impossible to navigate through the crowd. The deafening commotion resounded off the walls.

Physicians worked at a makeshift clinic on the balcony, away from the uproar. Nurses assisted them in the assessment of sick babies. Some were diagnosed too ill for travel and were sent to local hospitals for treatment.

Two hours later, the escorts gathered the children to board the plane. One by one babies and older children were taken through the back door of the plane and placed in their original seats by a volunteer, who then exited the front.

Mai rested her head back against the seat and took a deep breath as a force pulled the plane off the runway and her into a world unknown.

Before long she felt the weight of someone heavy plop into the seat beside her. She looked into Ross' bespectacled, smiling face. His hair was mussed, his shirt wrinkled, but his tired eyes still danced with a contagious merriment.

"Hi!"

"Hi," Mai grinned.

Ross soared his hand in the air and his mustache quivered as he imitated the sound of the plane engine. Mai giggled.

"No more Vietnam," he said, pointing out the window, shaking his head sadly.

The smile vanished from Mai's face. "No Vietnam," she repeated, shaking her head in time with his.

"America!" Ross exclaimed raising both arms over his head. Mai chuckled at his gestures, then shrugged and shook her head slowly again.

"America," Ross repeated. "To your daddy."

Drumming his fingers on the back of the seat, he looked around the plane as if scouting for help. He waved to a Vietnamese woman walking down the aisle with a baby in each arm. He took one of the infants from her and jostled it for her while they jabbered in the language Mai couldn't understand.

The woman crouched next to Mai. "Do you know where you are going?" she asked in her native tongue.

Mai simply shook her head and said, "No Vietnam."

"That's right." The woman squeezed her hand. "You are going to America." Mai shrugged again, wishing she understood the importance of this word everyone seemed so proud to recite.

Ross talked rapidly to the woman while he bounced the baby on his knee.

The Vietnamese woman continued. "Do you remember the America man that came to visit you all those years in Vietnam? Pete lives in America."

Mai nodded furiously and stared into the woman's eyes hoping the next sentence spoken would be the words she had longed to hear for seven years.

"We are taking you to him. Pete will be your daddy."

Mai jumped out of her seat and wrapped her arms around the woman's neck. She danced in place and clapped her hands then twirled, facing Ross. He chuckled as he pulled her up onto his unoccupied knee. She hugged him and the baby he was holding.

"My daddy!" she squealed, gesturing out the window. Then pointing to her chest she said, "Mai daddy."

Ross joined in her rollicking giggles, then placed her gently back into her own seat and returned to care for the babies in his charge a few rows back.

The plane lights dimmed in a futile attempt to cue its passengers it was time for sleep. Most of the infants couldn't be fooled and the adults continued the marathon of care. The older children, whose behavior at the airport had made the clowns seem subdued, were slowly lulled into inactivity.

The smile on Mai's face seemed as fixed as the clown's as she rested her head back on the soft seat. She recalled the many nights she had cried into her pillow at the orphanage and prayed for that special man, Pete, to return for her. She thought she felt her heart skip a beat as she tried to grasp the possibility that her dream was about to come true.

Any notion of sleep was dashed by daydreams of seeing her "daddy" in "America".

Hours later breakfast was served. An excitement she had never known raced through her blood and apparently her feet as she and her fellow traveling companions raced in the aisles of the plane. The only time Mai could remember being this happy was when she had been with Pete in Vietnam. She found Michael and engaged him and two other new friends in a game of hide-and-seek. The cockpit seemed an ideal place to hide, but crewmembers didn't seem to agree as they ushered her back to the cabin with grumpy expressions on their faces.

Her escort found her sampling the food cart and gestured for her to follow him to their seats and prepare for landing. She could hardly sit still as he fastened her seat belt and motioned for her to stay put. She bounced up and down as she anticipated living out her many daydreams.

CHAPTER 15

Connie stood on the runway of Travis Air Force base staring into the heavens. Shielding her eyes from the glaring California sun, she squinted at what she hoped was the plane carrying MaiLy and the other orphans. The task of organizing accommodations and paper work for hundreds of children had consumed her nights and days. She had been almost relieved to leave Denver, but found the same mountains of paperwork and pressures from the media waiting for her at the Presidio in San Francisco.

"How many babies do you expect on this flight, Mrs. Mason?" A female reporter jammed a microphone into Connie's face while a cameraman hoisted a video recorder onto his shoulder.

"Hopefully 300," Connie answered with a fake politeness. "I don't have many details since the government has taken over the airlift and entry of the children into the United States."

The resulting red tape and record keeping had been overwhelming.

"Is it true your adopted ten-year-old daughter is on this flight?"

Connie stared at her; amazed anyone had learned the well-kept secret.

"I don't know," she answered coolly.

Her fatigue from only two hours sleep a night had dissipated when she learned FVNC's first flight of orphans was expected mid-morning. Communication with her staff in the Philippines had been nearly impossible due to the magnitude of the airlift project there. She could only hope that Mai was on this plane.

How she wished Pete could be with her when MaiLy arrived. Because the situation in Denver remained chaotic, they agreed he should stay home to offer some stability and order for their two daughters. She had talked to him several times a day during the three days she'd been at the Presidio. Together, they had endured the labor of waiting the arrival of their next child.

Connie jerked her head in the direction of a hum in the distant sky and watched as the plane came into view and circled the airstrip.

"God, please let Mai be on this plane," she whispered. "After seven years, don't make us wait any more."

The jet taxied down the runway and came to a halt near where she stood. She noticed a passenger window shade rapidly moving up and down. Straining her eyes, she watched it finally snap up. There was Ross's familiar smile. She ran closer to the plane and watched as he mouthed, "We got her. We got Mai!"

"He's got her!" Connie yelled. Then turning to the flock of surprised reporters she hollered. "He's got her!"

She tapped her toes on the pavement and clutched the wrapped gift in her hands as she stared at the plane door. Eventually it opened and a haggard-looking flight attendant forced a smile. Connie couldn't help but chuckle imagining the most bizarre flight he had ever experienced.

An American woman appeared in the doorway and cautiously descended the steps carrying babies in both arms. Following her was a procession of exuberant but exhausted volunteers holding babies or toddlers. Reporters jogged along side them flashing questions and camera bulbs.

Connie elbowed her way through the crowd declaring, "No more questions. No more questions, please!"

She greeted the escorts and directed them onto the chartered bus. Dozens more men and women exited with children before Connie saw Ross standing alone in the doorway. Her heart ached momentarily, and then she saw Mai peer from behind him. She suppressed her urge to run and smother her with hugs and kisses.

Ross beamed as he coaxed Mai down the stairs holding her hand and leading her to her adoptive mother.

When Mai got within ten feet of Connie, she stopped, frozen. Connie went to her, stooped, and hugged her, but Mai wiggled loose, pushing her away. Connie and Ross looked to each other for explanation.

"She must be so scared and confused," Connie offered, "The only time she saw me before, I was with Pete. I wonder if she remembers me."

She extended the gift to Mai who abruptly folded her arms and set her chin in a pout.

"I don't know what's wrong," Ross said. "We were the last ones off the plane because she was laughing and running with the other kids."

Connie reached for Mai's hand but she snapped it away. Ross took it gently and led her onto the bus. He placed her in a seat then Connie sat beside her. When Connie tried to touch her, Mai angrily shoved her away. Placing both feet on the seat Mai began kicking madly, flailing her arms, and screaming.

Connie moved to the seat behind her and sat next to Ross. "I've never seen her like this," he apologized.

"And after all these years, I've seen everything," Connie mused. "She's not just sad, she's mad! Apparently, I'm not the person she was hoping to see."

Ross reached over the seat to console her but MaiLy slapped his arm away, bellowing and kicking furiously. She quit long enough to glare over the back of the seat. Connie smiled sweetly, but made no attempt to touch her. Mai spit, but the saliva only drooled down her chin. This seemed to heighten her anger, and she spun around and belted the seat in front of her again.

As the bus crossed the Golden Gate Bridge, the driver played tour guide, pointing out the island of Alcatraz to the escorts. The sun was setting over the bay and the breeze blew its warmth through the open windows. Connie stood and thanked the volunteers then explained to them the procedure for checking the children in at the Presidio.

When the bus stopped in front of the military building, the escorts began marching off with the children in tow. Connie reached for Mai's hand, but she slapped it away. Connie exited the bus and motioned for Ross to follow. When he did, Mai stomped down the steps behind him. Remembering how she loved presents and pretty clothes, Connie opened the gift she was carrying and handed Mai a red and blue sweater. Mai jerked it out of her hands and threw it on the ground. Connie scooped it up, smiled, put her arm around Ross's waist and walked slowly toward the building. As Mai shuffled along behind them, Connie teased, "You don't think this is any indication of what my relationship will be with my new daughter, do you Ross?"

The Presidio's interior was large enough to house the plane they had arrived on. Instead of neat rows of mattresses like at Clark Air Force Base, randomly placed mats covered the entire surface of the floor. Hundreds of children from a half-dozen agency were waiting to be processed. There was no place to walk through the sea of babbling toddlers and crying babies. The adults were yelling also to be heard above the din.

Mai finally grabbed Connie's hand as they tiptoed through the chaos. Connie plowed their way and Ross followed to the FVNC Headquarters table against the wall. Two women there greeted them and bent down to welcome Mai. She shook her head and stepped behind Connie. When one of the ladies tried to take her hand, Mai dropped to the floor kicking and swinging her arms.

"Cha! Cha!" she sobbed. All attempts Connie and Ross made to comfort her only increased the wailing pitch of her repeated cry.

"She's not mad, now, Ross." Connie choked. "She's heartbroken. Get the Vietnamese interpreter." Within minutes, the woman appeared.

"What is she saying," Connie pleaded.

"Cha is Vietnamese for father," the woman answered.

"Tell her we will take her to him soon."

The woman chattered to Mai while helping her into a sitting position on the floor. Mai buried her face in the woman's shoulder, talking and crying.

"She doesn't believe you. She thinks you tricked her into coming here and wants you to take her back to Vietnam. She feels kidnapped."

"Please make her understand," Connie begged. "In a few days we will take her to see Pete. He is waiting for her."

At the mention of Pete's name, Mai's crying was reduced to a whimper. Connie grabbed her purse and rummaged through it until she found her wallet. She hastily sorted through credit cards and grocery receipts.

"Here!" She presented a photo to Mai and sat beside her on the floor. "This is Mai and her daddy and me in Vietnam."

Mai wiped her nose with the back of her hand and took the photo.

Connie's finger moved over the picture. "Daddy, Mai, and me, Mommy." The last word stuck in her throat. A smile crossed Mai's lips and she looked up at Connie, who could only nod. Mai bantered back and forth with the translator then sat still, staring at the photo. Then she reached for Connie's hand, placed it in her lap, and smiled up at her.

"I love you," Connie said. "I've wanted you every bit as much as your daddy did." The Vietnamese woman repeated the phrase. Mai's grin illuminated her face.

They sat in silence a few minutes until Connie said, "Let me take some time to show her around." She stood, still clutching her daughter's hand. "Maybe I can make her feel a little more at home until we really get her home."

The Vietnamese woman darted off toward the sound of another tearful traveler as Connie led Mai toward the kitchen at the far end of the facility. There they ate and smiled, appreciating those universal languages. Next Connie took her upstairs where boxes of clothes lay strewn around the huge room. She let Mai pick out an outfit without mentioning that the plaid pants were too short and didn't match the flowered top she selected.

Back downstairs; they walked past a room full of cribs. Mai pulled Connie into the room and walked from crib to crib cooing to the infant occupants. Connie persuaded her to follow her to the adjoining room filled with children her age listening to a story. When Mai saw Michael there, she ran and wedged her way between him and the boy at his side. She wrapped her arms around him, then turned and waved good-bye to Connie.

Chuckling, Connie said to the Vietnamese reader, "Tell her I'm right out here working if she needs me." When that was translated, Mai smiled and nodded, nestling closer to Michael.

Within the hour, Connie saw Mai and Michael running wildly between the mats of dozing children. When they caught the unspoken warning in Connie's expression, they walked at a controlled pace past her table, then resumed their race through the crowd.

Connie turned to her coworker. "I'd say she's adjusting rather well, wouldn't you?"

CHAPTER 16

Mai's eyes popped open when she heard the babies crying. A familiar sadness enveloped her when she realized the sound was not coming from the nursery at Domani de Marie. She lay still so she wouldn't wake Michael sleeping on the mat beside her.

Recollections of her confusion and fear the day before made her feel anxious again. Were people telling her the truth now? Would they really take her to see her daddy soon? The lady with the red hair did seem to care about her. When Mai had woke in the night, she found her new mother cuddled beside her, stroking her cheek. Mai felt shame for the way she had kicked her yesterday. She had never behaved like that before. If she had acted that way at the orphanage, she would be sleeping with the chickens again. After years of strict discipline, it was exciting, now, to have the freedom to misbehave. A sly smile matched her mischievous eyes as she imagined the escapades awaiting her today.

Michael woke and accompanied her to breakfast with her mother, who hugged Mai every time she spoke. Then she and Michael were taken to their assigned area and encouraged to participate in the games and activities there. After an hour of supervised play, Mai motioned for Michael and several other boys and girls to follow her out of the room.

Connie sat behind piles of papers in the cubicle office assigned her. She had enjoyed breakfast with Mai and wished she could spend the day with her, but the volumes of paper work chained her to her desk. A heap of forms had served as a pillow while she slept an hour during the night. Several staff members from Denver had offered to come help her trudge through the paper trail, but she declined their offers insisting it was easier to do it alone.

"It would take me longer to explain it to someone than to do it myself," she reassured Pete when they spoke on he phone. "If I can just have a few days without interruption, I can get this done and come home."

He had delighted in the details of Mai's arrival and admitted he, too, was surprised at her behavior.

"Now that she understands what's going on, I'm sure she'll be fine," he promised.

A knock at the door swung it open. "Mai has formed a gang and is running all over this place!" an American volunteer blurted. "They're running and yelling and won't stay in the room with the others."

I'd better nip this in the bud, Connie thought. She followed the volunteer to where Mai stood cornered by several adults. When she saw Connie, she flashed an engaging smile and stroked the red and blue sweater she was wearing.

"I'm glad you like the present now," Connie said with the help of an interpreter, "but you must obey the rules. You must stay in the room with the other children."

Mai nodded demurely and Connie went back to work.

She was typing furiously when she heard a tap, tap, and tap on the top of her desk. She glanced up at Mai, then finished the thought she was constructing on paper.

Tap, tap, tap. It was louder now.

Bam, bam, bam. Mai struck her fist on the desk.

Connie stopped her work and stared into Mai's smiling face -- and extended palm.

"Change," Mai said in perfect English.

"What?" Connie couldn't help but laugh.

"Change," Mai repeated just as a frustrated worker huffed into the room.

"I'm sorry, Connie. She got away from us again and is fascinated with the pop machine in the entryway. She learned fast how to ask for money, and when we wouldn't give her any, she ran to you."

Mai's smile broadened as her eyes pleaded.

Connie chuckled and took a quarter from the top drawer. She walked around her desk and hugged her daughter. "Here," she said, "but no more."

Her sentence was left incomplete as Mai snatched the coin from her hand and raced out the door, the volunteer close behind.

An hour later an American soldier appeared at her desk. "Mrs. Mason, are you the one in charge here?"

Connie sighed and glanced at him then resumed her work. "Yes, but could someone else help you? I'm on over-load right now."

"We caught a group of kids breaking into a pop machine."

Another soldier ushered four boys and Mai into the room.

Connie slapped her pencil down on the desk and groaned. "What's going on?"

"Certain areas of this facility are off limits to unauthorized personnel. Metal gates have been erected to prevent access to these areas. These, these - - children scaled those eight foot fences and bashed in the fronts of two pop machines and confiscated an unspecified number of cans."

Mai smiled sheepishly in response to Connie's glare.

"I really don't have time for this."

The same Vietnamese interpreter hustled into the room.

Connie huffed, "Tell these kids that if they don't quit breaking the rules, I'm going to have this soldier put them under guard!"

The soldier looked worried, so Connie muttered, "I'm only kidding." She heaved a sigh and plopped into her chair. To the interpreter she said, "Take them back to their assigned room and warn them they'd better stay there." Shaking her pencil at Mai, she repeated, "I don't have time for this. We'll never get home if you keep causing trouble and I have all these interruptions."

The interpreter repeated the admonition as she herded the group out the door. Mai looked over her shoulder, performing her perfected pout as she exited.

Thirty minutes later another soldier appeared. "Mrs. Mason, we need you in the infirmary."

"You're going to have to handle it yourself this time. I can't leave."

"One of the children is causing a panic situation in the medical complex, Ma'am," the soldier reported.

Slamming her folder down, Connie shoved her chair away from her desk and into the wall behind her.

"Now what?'

"Follow me, please. I'll explain on the way."

Moaning, Connie stood and followed him out of the room and through the bedlam of babies.

"You are aware of regulations requiring every orphan to have a blood test upon arrival into the country?" the Private shouted. Connie nodded impatiently. She could hear the shrieking and crying as they neared the infirmary. Inside, the walls rattled with the sound of two dozen toddlers and older children wailing in unison. Cheeks puffed and eyes squinted as tears streaked every face.

A new volunteer hustled toward her.

"If this weren't so pathetic, it would be funny," Connie hollered above the roar. "What the heck is going on here?"

"We gathered all the toddlers and older kids, including Mai, into the clinic to get their fingers poked for the blood tests. Everything was fine, but suddenly all twenty-some of them started bawling and screaming at the same time. I mean, it was deafening, all of them crying at once. We kept asking them what was wrong, but they only bawled louder. Finally, the interpreter got the story from one of the kids. It seems once the kids were all corralled in here, Mai announced to them, in Vietnamese, of course, that if their fingers were poked they would die immediately! That's when they all started screaming. And who could blame them?"

Connie's face reddened and she spit out the words, "Where is she?"

The volunteer gestured to where Mai sat giggling with her friends.

"Bring her to the front of the room and sit her on the table," Connie barked. "And get the doctor with the blood test ready."

When Mai saw Connie stomp toward the table with gritted teeth, she wiped the grin off her face with her hand.

To the interpreter Connie said, "Tell all of them to stop crying. They aren't going to die."

The Vietnamese woman shouted the phrases over and over until the wailing became sniveling whimpers. By now, Mai was grinning again.

"Repeat after me," Connie instructed the translator.

"Children, the blood test is not bad for you, it is good for you." The translator smiled and shook her head up and down with reassurance as she repeated the message.

"It is a tiny, finger stick but it hurts only for a second. You will not die," Connie said emphatically. "And we can prove it to you now. Doctor?"

The physician wore a white coat and had a small lab tool in his hand. An anxious look replaced Mai's smile as Connie wrapped her arm around her in a bear hug. Then the volunteer braced her from the other side. Together, they held her hand in front of the doctor. He poked her finger with a lancet and within seconds filled a micro-tube with a few drops of blood while Mai yelped and kicked.

Connie released her, and then turned to the other children with both arms extended toward Mai. "She lives!" she exclaimed and walked out of the room.

"Sure, it's easy for you to laugh, Pete. You're not here putting up with her!" Connie chuckled into the phone that evening.

"Now, now, Honey," Pete cajoled, "You know you love her as much as I do."

"Of course I do, " Connie said leaning back in her chair and putting her feet on the desk. "She's even more beautiful than her pictures. But her angelic face had a devilish grin. She's driving me nuts here."

"Nobody said it was going to be easy."

"Easy? You haven't heard the half of it yet. I'm right in the middle of filing the I-90 Humanitarian Visas and checking to be sure we have the required finger prints and blood tests on each kid, when a cook comes stomping into the room. It seems in the night Mai and her banditos snuck into the kitchen and stole all the meat and cheese from a few hundred sandwiches. Lots of people were disappointed with a mayonnaise sandwich today."

Pete was laughing. "How do they know it was her?"

"Apparently one of the banditos fessed up and tattled on her. Then Mai's bellyache confirmed the verdict."

"We all know it's common for orphans who were raised hungry to steal and horde food when they get here, but I have to say, this was a bit extreme," Pete mused.

"I know a nice family in Philadelphia who's looking for an older child."

"Oh no, you don't. Not after all we've been through!"

"Okay, okay. If I ever get all this paper work done, I'll bring her home to you."

"I'm sending Ted and Dick to help you..."

"No, Pete," Connie interrupted. "It's easier for me to do it myself."

"Connie, there's more work than one person can handle. Besides, I miss you and want you home soon. Let us help you."

"If you really want to help me, leave me alone."

They exchanged kisses, then Connie replaced the phone in the cradle. She looked at her watch. Two a.m. Finally a quiet time to get some work done.

CHAPTER 17

"The buses are here."

Connie jammed the last stack of files into a box. "Then let's go." She took a final look around the room that had served as her Presidio office and dorm room. "I want FVNC's quarters here completely evacuated by noon."

"What's the rush?" the worker asked as she helped lug cartons down the hall.

"Three days here with MaiLy and her gang is three too many," Connie chuckled. The volunteer grinned and waited for the real answer.

"We've tried to keep the news about the bomb threats here a secret," Connie whispered. "They've all checked out negative, but we don't want to press our luck or panic everybody."

It was incomprehensible to imagine how anyone could threaten the lives of children she and others had worked so hard to save. Hating a war was one thing, but threatening the lives of its victims--the children--was another, beyond her understanding.

In the two weeks Connie had been at the Presidio, over two hundred babies had been sent to their pre-assigned homes. Now the remaining one hundred toddlers and older children would be flown to Denver and housed temporarily in a newly built, still-unoccupied nursing home until final placements were made.

Outside she watched as Red Cross and military volunteers escorted children onto the chartered buses headed to the airport. Shouts from a Vietnamese interpreter disrupted the orderly commotion. Connie rushed to ask, "What's the problem here?" She saw Mai and Michael clinging to each other, wailing. The interpreter explained that the two said they were siblings and this process was splitting them up.

"They are not siblings." Connie rolled her eyes. "They just met last week!"

The interpreter shook her head at Mai who immediately quit crying to scowl at Connie. Mai slapped Connie's extended hand and took the fingers of her escort as she stomped up the stairs of the bus. Exasperated, Connie grasped her clipboard to her chest, and hustled to the second bus to make sure the assigned children were on board.

After a flight that harried all escorts and flight attendants, they arrived at Denver's Stapleton International Airport. Officials there were aware of previous bomb threats; so all the children and adults were shepherded through a tunnel to avoid attention in the terminal. From there, another bus ride to Continental Care Nursing home.

The cold April wind blew Mai to Connie's side as they approached the newly built nursing home. Clinging tightly to her hand, Mai ascended a flight of stairs to the second story medical unit where each child would receive yet another government-required exam.

Connie pushed the stairwell door open. At the very moment Pete came rushing toward them. Mai shook loose of her hand and ran to Pete shouting, "Cha! Cha!" He stooped and swept her into his arms, twirling her around and around as she clutched his neck in their familiar hug.

"I can't believe you're finally here," he breathed as Mai wiped tears from his cheeks. He opened one arm and Connie stepped into the embrace. "This is all I ever wanted." Mai nestled her face into his shoulder. "Mai daddy," she whispered. She wouldn't let Pete out of her sight.

The interpreter explained that Pete and Connie had to help with the dozens of other children still arriving, but Mai followed on his heels with an incessant grin plastered on her face. Pete assembled the youngsters in the medical office with Mai beside him, imitating his every move. When he tried to walk across the room, Mai sat on his foot and clung to his thigh. She tossed her head back and laughed from her belly. Pete dropped to his knees and they rocked in each other's arms, oblivious to the commotion around them.

Because the children had undergone exams in Vietnam, the Philippines, Hawaii, and the Presidio, they had the routine memorized. When an attendant in a white lab coat directed them to the exam table, they immediately stuck out their tongues then pulled their ear lobes, tilting their heads to one side. The new building rocked with the trampling and laughter of several hundred children and bustling volunteers.

The community had responded to radio and TV requests for assistance. An outpouring of compassion, money, and volunteers welcomed the new arrivals. The University of Colorado medical school provided physicians and nursing staff to perform the required exams and necessary treatments. Caring citizens tended the rooms of children, divided by age. Others assisted with the preparation and serving of Vietnamese meals.

Mai watched as adoptive parents met the children they had labored for and loved for so many months. Adults and children wept as they hugged new members of their families for the first time.

It was nearly dark outside when Mai finally dozed sitting upright with her head resting against the wall. A gentle tap on her shoulder woke her and she squinted into Pete's adoring blue eyes. Lifting her into his strong arms, he said, "Come, MaiLy. Time to go."

"I wish I could go with you," Connie said as she draped a jacket over Mai's shoulders. "I'll probably be here most of the night getting all the kids processed. I'll try to be home by morning when she meets her sisters."

"This isn't exactly how I had pictured Mai's homecoming," Pete admitted. "But it's hard to plan when you're in the middle of an emergency airlift." Then putting an arm around his wife he whispered, "I miss you." Kissing her cheek he added, "but I understand and love you for all you're doing."

They shared another kiss, then he bundled Mai into his arms and said, "Daddy's going to take you home."

CHAPTER 18

Mai clung to Pete's hand as he led her out of the chaos and into the quiet suburban Denver night. A late spring snowfall had begun silently blanketing the dormant earth. Mai stopped, staring at the snow glistening under the streetlight.

The bewildered look on her face made Pete chuckle. "Snow." He scooped some into his hand and repeated, "Snow."

Mai touched it then jerked her hand away, stung by the cold. Slowly, she reached to the ground and poked the white powder with her fingertip. Giggling, she scooped both hands full and tossed the shimmering crystals into the air. Pete did the same. "Snow!"

"Snow!" Mai echoed.

He warmed her hand in his as he guided her to a blue van. Only now did she realize the real purpose of her journey. The feelings of abduction and confusion were replaced by a happiness she'd never known. As they passed rows and rows of houses and stores, Mai recalled their outings together in Vietnam. The unfamiliar flashing signs and lights filled her with excitement not worry. Somehow, being with her daddy, things were sure to be safe and good. She nestled closer to him and returned his loving smile.

The van stopped in front of a two-story house. Pete led her up the cobblestone path and unlocked the ornate wooden door. Mai's eyes widened as she gazed around the living room with its plush furniture and beautiful decor.

"Nha," Pete said. "Home."

Mai grinned.

Taking her hand, he showed her the downstairs rooms, turning lights on as they went. Polished wooden floors and stair banisters held no resemblance to those at Domani de Marie. Green houseplants, colorful walls, braided rugs, and ornate lamps mystified her. Pete continued to speak to her in the language she did not understand, but she knew she was in the home she had prayed for all these years.

One room had lots of toys. *Maybe children live here,* Mai thought. Pete took her to the couch next to the window. She cuddled close to him and rested her head on his chest while they sat in silence watching the snowfall. Icy snowflakes on the windowpane glistened in kaleidoscopic colors under the porch light.

Sister Katrine had been right.

There are rainbows at the end of the storms.

Mai woke in the early morning sunlight, her head on a pillow in Pete's lap. Over the past few weeks she had wakened in many different surroundings and was accustomed to feeling a little afraid and confused. Now, a new feeling of safety and joy chased away her initial anxiety. She lay there awhile enjoying the sound of her daddy's light snore and the touch of his hand on her arm.

Muffled sounds of children talking and laughing lured her to her feet and into the adjoining room. She followed the noise down a flight of stairs but stopped abruptly at the bottom and gawked. Toys lay strewn around the floor and furniture.

A girl, about Mai's size, ran to her and pulled her into the middle of the room. She had yellow hair, blue eyes, and pink cheeks that got rounder when she smiled.

"Marcie." She drummed her chest, then jumped in place and squealed with delight. Another littler girl with yellow hair sat at a child-size table coloring. "Erica," Marcie said pointing to her. The little girl didn't wave or smile, but scribbled even harder.

Just then Pete appeared at the foot of the stairs. Mai raced to him, clinging to his waist.

"Gia dinh," he said waving his hand around the room. "Family."

He squatted and extended his arms wide. "Family!" On cue, the blonde girls ran to his embrace just as Connie descended the stairs and joined them.

A family hug, with Mai in the middle.

Connie clapped her hands and said, "Better get ready for school. I'll take you on my way back to work."

Erica grasped her mom's hand and jumped up the stairs one at a time. "I'm glad you're home from California, Mommy. We missed you."

"And I missed all of you so much," Connie said, kissing the top of the child's curly head.

"Will you come home for supper?" Erica asked with a final jump.

"I'll try, Sweetie. Mommy has lots and lots of babies and little kids to find homes for."

"They can come here," Marcie offered, as she coaxed Mai into a chair at the kitchen table.

Connie and Pete laughed. "That's nice of you to offer, Honey, but 200 kids wouldn't fit here very well. Besides, each of them is in a hurry to go to their own families."

"Like MaiLy!" Marcie chirped.

Mai smiled at the mention of her name.

Pete walked around the table filling each bowl with Cheerios and Connie followed with a pitcher of milk. Marcie sprinkled sugar on Mai's cereal, then her own. Mai's eyes lit and her smile broadened when she tasted the sweet breakfast. Giggling between spoonfuls, she gobbled the rest.

"Can I take Mai to school for show-and-tell?" Marcie begged. "I'll have the best in all second grade!"

"Kindergartners have show-and-tell, too," Erica objected. "Can I take her tomorrow?"

"You'll have to just tell, not show, for now," Connie said, "Mai needs some time to be with just us first. She'll come with me to the care center for a few days. That way she can be close to me but also be with other kids and grown-ups who can speak Vietnamese. Mai's been through a lot the past few weeks. There will be people there who can talk to her and help her adjust to all this."

When they finished eating, Marcie and Erica placed their bowls and spoons in the dishwasher, then Marcie led Mai upstairs.

"This is our room," she boasted. Mai's eyes danced from the Mickey Mouse bedspreads to the matching wall decorations. She turned in a circle in the middle of the room, her grin as big as Mickey's.

"Do you want the top bunk or the bottom bunk?" Marcie asked, pointing to each like a game show host. "This dresser is full of new clothes, just for you!" she exclaimed, opening the drawers one at a time. "I think you should wear this."

Marcie helped Mai in and out of several different outfits before Connie called up the stairs announcing Mom's taxi was about to leave. The girls thundered down the stairs, donned their jackets, and hustled to the family van. Marcie directed Mai through the routine and buckled her into the seat belt.

"This will be the best show-and-tell yet!"

CHAPTER 19

"Like this!" Marcie coached as she sucked the strand of spaghetti into her mouth at supper. The rest of the family laughed as Mai copied her, the dangling end of the noodle smearing red sauce across her cheeks. The girls began a contest to see who could suck the longest strand without stopping. Pete and Connie looked on, smiling, until Marcie began singing, "On top of spaghetti all covered with cheese." That's when Pete said that would be enough and they'd have to settle down and eat now.

"Mai's going to think we're all a little goofy," Pete said, winking at MaiLy. Squinting one eye, then the other, she returned the wink.

"You can be sure mealtime at the orphanage was never like this," Pete added. "The nuns were very strict. Besides slurping spaghetti, we'll have lots to teach her."

"That's why I put our signs up today, all over the house." Marcie motioned to the cards taped on dozens of kitchen objects. Each item had the English and Vietnamese word for it printed in big letters.

Marcie pointed to the card taped on the table next to Mai. "See, MaiLy? Cai ban -- table."

Mai nodded and grinned. "Table," she enunciated perfectly.

Marcie clapped and Erica joined in a round of applause. Next, Marcie pointed to the sign on the back of Mai's chair. "Ghe -- chair."

"Chair," Mai beamed.

"Glass," Erica said, raising hers.

"Glass," Mai repeated. Everyone lifted theirs simultaneously. "Glass!" they chorused.

The parroting continued until each piece of tableware and every kitchen appliance had been identified. When the meal finally ended, Mai joined the others in rinsing the dishes and placing them in the dishwasher.

Marcie and Erica went downstairs to play while Mai joined Pete on the sofa. He handed her a book with a ribbon around it. They cuddled together to read the children's' Vietnamese/ English picture-book dictionary. Mai read each Vietnamese word fluently then eagerly attempted it in English. She seemed disappointed when, two hours later, Pete announced it was bedtime.

Marcie led Mai upstairs and gleefully showed her the new nightgown on her bed. "First, we have to take a shower," Marcie groaned. Mai followed her to the bathroom, but refused to enter the shower stall. She stood firmly, and shook her head until Marcie stepped in to prove its safety. Then Marcie showered and exited, smiling. Mai stood rigidly. Next, Connie helped Erica into the shower. She splashed and giggled then jumped out to enjoy a hug from Connie as she bundled her in the towel. Only then did Mai take her turn, huddling in the corner of the stall.

She was obviously perplexed by the teeth-brushing demonstration, but obediently complied, wedging the foamy brush over her teeth for the first time.

Marcie decided Mai would prefer the bottom bunk. She tucked her under the blankets and kissed her cheek before climbing the ladder to her bed. The Mickey Mouse night-light provided just enough light for her to see Mai sneak out from under the covers and kneel next to the bed -- back straight, hands folded.

For the next few weeks Mai accompanied Connie to the care center each day. Thuy taught classes of Vietnamese culture for the children and their adoptive parents. Mai enjoyed spending time with Michael and connecting with her past, and was surprised to realize she missed the people and routines that had guided her life in Vietnam. Counselors at the care center reminded her she could mourn the loss of her past and at the same time celebrate the goodness of the present.

As her confidence increased during her days at the center, so did her boredom. Pulling the forbidden fire alarm provided a great distraction and entertainment. The deafening shrill spurred workers to hustle about, closing doors and shouting to each other.

"Who planned a fire drill?" one volunteer hollered.

Mai giggled as she scurried to blend in with the other children. Toddlers started crying and babies joined in. Just when the grown-ups calmed them to a quiet, sirens roared on the streets. Then Mai and the older children screamed, haunted by the memories those sounds represented. Trembling, they watched out the window as fire trucks and police cars approached.

"They came to help us, not hurt us," Michael explained. "They think there's a fire here."

Mai stopped crying and gave Michael a sly grin.

The firefighters, dressed in their black boots and yellow slickers, entered the building. Mai and her friends flocked around them, caught up in the excitement.

Connie and the other adults didn't share in it, however.

"Who pulled the fire alarm?" she called out, then under her breath she muttered, "as if I didn't know."

All eyes, from every adult, child, and toddler seemed to rest on Mai.

She smiled her sweetest smile and shrugged.

Sitting alone in Connie's office for the rest of the day only heightened her boredom.

Mai appreciated being able to talk to other children at the center in Vietnamese, but enjoyed even more trying to talk to her sisters at the end of the day. Marcie loved playing school as soon as she got home each day. She was always the self-appointed teacher, and drilled Mai and Erica on lessons in English and numbers. Mai loved the undivided attention and caught on to the new language quickly.

Marcie usually announced recess about thirty minutes before supper. Mai loved playing in the sandbox and on the swing set. When Pete came home, he could barely get through the gate before the girls jumped into his arms, laughing along with him.

Mai soon learned the mealtime routine and took her turn setting the table, identifying each item in English as she did. When she cleared the table and loaded the dishwasher, she repeated the exercise. Marcie beamed like a proud teacher.

As the May sunsets lingered, there was more time to play outside after supper. One warm, balmy evening, Marcie and Erica were summoned inside to clean up a mess, so Mai swung alone on the swing set. She breathed deeply the fresh spring air and looked around at the lush green lawn and flowers blooming near the fence. She felt like Cinderella in the book Marcie had read. Images of the dirt playground at Domani de Marie crept into her mind. How could she love this beautiful place so much, and still miss the drab and lonely orphanage? Sometimes during quiet nights, she scolded herself for longing for her life in Vietnam.

The porch screen door squeaked and Pete came to join her in the yard. He lifted Mai from the swing, then sat in it, placing her on his lap. She could wrap her arms almost completely around his chest, now. She rested her head on his shoulder. In perfect English she said, "Mai daddy. Mai's home. Mai happy."

CHAPTER 20

It took Mai awhile to realize that when Marcie talked about Mai going to school, she wasn't talking about their playtime together.

Marcie laid Mai's new dress on the bed and talked of teachers, classmates, and lesson assignments as she bounced around the room. She reminded Mai of Tigger in another book they'd been reading together.

At breakfast, Connie and Pete confirmed the plan. This was to be Mai's first day of school. The sugared cereal didn't settle very well with all the excitement and fear wrestling inside her.

She joined the family in packing an extra lunch. Clutching it in one hand, and Pete's hand in the other, she joined her siblings in the walk to school.

Dozens more children paraded alongside them as they neared the building. A loud bell sounded, and the pace of the march quickened. Mai had been here once before, for Marcie's show-and-tell day. Marcie had gloated in front of the class, holding Mai's hand, patting her head, and chattering rapidly. The other children approached Mai and pawed and patted her. She hoped every school day was not like that.

She squeezed Pete's hand tighter as he led her through a hallway lined with brightly colored, hand-drawn pictures and crowded with kids laughing and talking too loudly. He took her into a room of about twenty boys and girls tossing things into their wooden desks and slamming them closed.

"This is Mrs. Lawton, your teacher," Pete said. Her hair was brown and curly, with a little bit of gray on top. Her smile made Mai feel welcomed and more at ease. Mai took her hand and bowed slightly.

Pete pointed to the clock on the wall, then pointed to the number three on the watch Mai was wearing. He had given it to her the week before and together -- with Marcie too, of course -- they had been working on telling time. He pointed to the three on his watch and said he'd be back then to get her. He kissed her cheek lightly as the other kids stared. Then he left.

Suddenly the room was very quiet.

"This is MaiLy," Mrs. Lawton said. "She is from Vietnam."

The kids continued to stare, and Mai was relieved when Mrs. Lawton directed her to a desk near the window. All eyes followed her as she took her seat.

Mrs. Lawton went to the front of the room and began reading names of the students, one at a time. After each name, someone answered, "Here." Mai tried to remember some of the names, but they sounded too unfamiliar to memorize. Then Mrs. Lawton said, "MaiLy."

"Here!" Mai shouted spontaneously. The students yelped and hollered and clapped. She could feel her face getting red and wanted to hide it in her desk. Mrs. Lawton said something in a loud voice, and the students quieted immediately, then took books from their desks. Mai found a matching one in hers and smiled when she recognized it as a geography text. That had been one of her favorite subjects in

Vietnam, and a source of some of her best classroom daydreams.

Now here she was in a part of the world she had once only fantasized about.

The girl next to her opened Mai's book to the appropriate page and Mai tried to follow along as classmates took turns reading aloud. She recognized only a few of the words. *Will I ever be able to understand this language?* She wondered. *Can I learn all that this and other books have to teach me?*

At recess, all the girls from class gathered around her on the playground. One held a ball and said very slowly, "Want to play ball?"

Another pointed to the long row of swings. "Want to swing?"

Mai noticed another classmate drawing with chalk on the sidewalk. She walked closer, with the other girls following behind her. When she saw the hopscotch pattern outlined, Mai jumped across the squares without stopping to consider what she was doing. The other girls squealed and clapped their hands. Mai could feel her face getting red again, but her new friends motioned for her to return across the course, then hugged her when she did. Mrs. Lawton looked on, smiling, as each girl took her turn.

The rest of the day went quickly as Mai tried to follow along in books she didn't understand. At lunch, Marcie sat at her table, easing MaiLy's confusion and frustration.

When Mrs. Lawton was writing on the chalkboard, the students talked and laughed and bustled about the room. Mai had never seen such behavior in a classroom. She stared out the window and daydreamed about school at Domani de Marie. There it was so still you could hear the nun's chalk screech across the chalkboard. She recalled standing alone for an hour in a corner as punishment for whispering in class.

"Quiet!" Mai heard herself shout.

Mrs. Lawton quit writing on the board and turned to stare.

The other students halted mid-sentence.

A hush fell over the classroom.

Then everyone could hear Mrs. Lawton's chalk screech across the board.

CHAPTER 21

Mai was grateful there were only four weeks of school before summer vacation. She grew tired and impatient with people who talked with a foreign language and hand gestures. She was intolerant of classmates who laughed whenever she spoke. She was bored with textbooks and classroom exercises she couldn't understand. She was frustrated and saddened by people who shook their heads when she tried to speak to them. As they walked home from the last day of school together, she vowed to Marcie that she would return in the fall reading, writing, and speaking English.

Her mom and dad had numerous opportunities lined up to help her meet that that goal. They worked with her in phonics workbooks and beginning readers. When Marcie wasn't playing teacher, Connie and Pete took turns reading with Mai. The local newspaper had a Kid's Page of games and puzzles on Saturdays. MaiLy raced to retrieve that edition as soon as it hit the lawn, so she could claim it first. The family spent countless hours playing board games, which Mai mastered quickly, and often won.

Mornings were spent doing regimented household chores. Daily tasks were written on index cards and each family member was assigned one on a rotating basis. MaiLy eagerly did her job and frequently nagged her siblings to do theirs. She was intolerant of clutter and poor care of possessions.

Afternoons were spent playing, riding bikes, and roller-skating. Undaunted by skinned knees, bruised shins, and scraped elbows, Mai got back on the wheels and practiced until she could keep up with the others. Several of her new friends from school lived nearby and their friendships grew over the summer.

The city pool proved to be a great gathering place for many of her friends and classmates. Each time they greeted Mai there, they complimented her increased ability to speak and understand English. With each accolade, Mai's confidence grew.

She enjoyed playing in the shallow water of the swimming pool, but refused to be coaxed into the deep end. When the ten-year-old boys splashed Mai and her friends and threatened to push them in, the other girls yelled and laughed and splashed them back. Mai tried to stay out of that type of play but couldn't avoid it one hot afternoon late in the summer.

Mai and her friends were floating on air mattresses in the shallow end of the pool when a team of boys began splashing water over them. The girls giggled and squealed in supposed protests. The louder the girls yelled, the larger the waves became.

So the boys rocked the plastic rafts wildly, threatening to over-turn them. The other girls sputtered and laughed and screamed.

But Mai only screamed.

Her hysteric shrill jolted the lifeguard to her feet, blasting her whistle.

"What's wrong with Mai?" the ornery boys yelled.

Mai clamored off her air mattress and stumbled to the side of the pool, coughing. Huddling next to the fence, she sat hugging herself, shivering, and crying. Marcie ran to her and stroked her hair saying, "It's okay, it's okay."

"Not okay!" Mai choked. "I almost die on raft!" She cried harder while the others looked on with sorrowful looks on their faces

"No, no, MaiLy," Marcie soothed. "You won't die here. It's only a swimming pool."

"No!" Mai shouted, then lowered her quivering voice and repeated. "I almost die on raft."

She knew Marcie didn't understand and questioned whether anyone ever would.

Mai enjoyed family camping trips in the mountains, though initially she found it peculiar that they would deliberately trade the luxuries of their city home for a deprived lifestyle. She quickly learned the family's favorite sing-a-long songs and glowed in the light of the campfire as she nestled next to her daddy. The family hikes, marshmallow roasts, and tent-pitching contests, drew her in deeply.

She lay under the stars one night and gazed at the same moon she had dreamed under in Vietnam. Sometimes she could hardly believe that dream had come true. Many mornings she was surprised, still, to wake and find she was no longer in the orphanage.

The whole family went to the park on the Fourth of July. She found Marcie's explanation of democracy fascinating and wondered if Sister Katrine and the others she left in Vietnam would ever know that freedom.

Pete and Connie told her about fireworks, the noise, the colors, and the excitement. Mai conceded that this was another one of those things she couldn't understand until she saw it.

Bands played all afternoon in the gazebo while thousands listened, danced, played ball, and ate watermelon.

Mai thought she could feel the freedom in the air and sensed all those celebrating could, too.

The sunset and the crowds quieted as the music became more serene.

Blankets were spread on the grass and the commotion and noise seemed to diminish with the daylight.

Obeying Marcie's instructions, Mai lay on the blanket next to her and Erica and watched the sky. She was intrigued, as usual, with the moon and stars when the first explosion fired. The sky lit with red and white streaks and a second blast seemed to break the heavens wide open. Mai jumped to her feet, shrieking, but didn't know where to run. Her scream didn't end, even when Pete grabbed her into his arms.

"It's okay, it's okay, it can't hurt you," he soothed while fireworks continued. Shaking, Mai covered her ears with her hands. Her mom joined in attempts to calm her, pointing out that Marcie and Erica weren't afraid. When Mai saw Marcie nodding and smiling, she stifled her sobs. Pete tried to explain the tradition above the blasting noise.

So Mai tried to be brave, as she and Pete watched the rest of the fireworks display, snuggled together under a picnic table.

The one place Mai felt safest was in church. She was astonished to see the familiar surroundings when she went to mass for the first time with her new family. Every aspect of her environment had been foreign to her until she entered the sanctuary. A familiar peace came over her as she walked down the center aisle, gawking at the marble altar, painted statues, and stained glass windows. So entranced was she, she didn't notice the rest of the family had slipped into a pew. Mai walked ahead, drawn to the statue of the Virgin Mary in the front. She looked up into the friendly face that had so often consoled her at Domani de Marie. Instinctively, she knelt before the statue, recalling the many times she had done so in Vietnam. All the prayers she had said before the statue there had been answered. "Cam on, Thoung de," she whispered. Then remembering her new life and language she said, almost giggling, "Thanks God."

When she stood to find her family, she was relieved to see Pete standing a few feet behind her. She thought she saw tears in his eyes as he led her back to her mom and sisters.

Another reason Mai liked church was because of its summer camp. She was glad that cutting, pasting, and making crafts did not require advanced language skills. Each morning, she joined the family in packing sack lunches, then Connie took the three girls to Bible School on her way to work. Mai often wished her parents could stay home with her, and wondered what they did away from the house all day. The nuns left the orphanage on rare occasions only. Connie told her that all the airlift children were placed in adoptive homes within thirty days, but the paperwork would keep her and her staff busy for many months.

After a morning of fun at church, the girls went to the neighbors across the street from them to spend the rest of the day. They didn't like the term "baby-sitter," so called Mrs. Riley their friend. She wasn't old enough to be a grandma, but acted like one, Marcie said. Baking cookies, playing games, and serving lemonade made the time with her pass too quickly. Mrs. Riley seemed especially fond of MaiLy and always talked slower and louder to her.

The Rileys' back yard seemed bigger and more spacious than the Mason's. Probably because it wasn't so full of bikes and toys, Mai guessed. As much as she had complained about fieldwork in Vietnam, she had to admit she found herself missing it here. It still baffled her how she missed the drab cot where she had slept, the stark tables where she had eaten, and the barren dirt where she had played-- and Minh. She missed Minh. Maybe that's why she enjoyed weeding Mrs. Riley's garden. She felt close to Minh there. Her sisters, and even Mrs. Riley shook their heads when Mai took off her sandals and worked barefoot in the dirt.

After supper Pete called up the stairs, "Who wants ice cream?"

Marcie was reviewing arithmetic problems with her best and only pupil.

"We do!" the girls chorused as they thundered down the steps. The whole family piled into the station wagon that appeared to have had too many treats eaten in it already. Connie looked back over the front seat at the three smiling faces and smiled too. She scooted to sit closer to Pete as they headed for the Dairy Queen.

Pete carefully carried a tray with five tall cones to the patio table where the girls oohed and aahed at the towering chocolate swirls. The hot summer air melted the ice cream faster than their twirling tongues could keep up. Soon Marcie, Erica, and Mai had sticky brown streaks running from their fists to their elbows to the table, where the goo formed puddles. The more Connie and Pete mopped, the quicker it melted.

"Try to eat faster," Pete coaxed patiently.

That's when the contest began.

The three girls licked madly, smearing ice cream over their chins and cheeks.

"Okay, settle down now," Connie said, stifling a grin.

But it was too late. The girls were laughing so hard they could hardly hold onto their cones. Moved by the spirit of the moment, Mai broke into her snorting pig routine, deliberately smashing her ice cream down her throat and up her nose.

"MaiLy!" Connie snapped the cone from her hands. "If that's how you're going to eat it, you can't have it."

She yanked napkins from the dispenser and rubbed too hard as she wiped the mess off Mai's face.

Marcie and Erica quieted immediately and Pete wiped their chins and arms with more napkins. Mai sat stunned and confused as she watched her sisters finish their cones without a word, while hers lay melting on the table.

All the scoldings from all the nuns had never made her feel as sad as this one.

Mai set her chin firmly, determined not to cry, and didn't speak all the way home.

CHAPTER 22

Connie planned several FVNC picnics over the summer. Mai loved going and seeing many of her friends from the airlift. She couldn't understand why she felt a special comfort when she was with other Vietnamese people. Sometimes she got that same feeling when she went with her mom to the Vietnamese market. She knew none of the people there, yet felt an acceptance that confused her. Occasionally at the picnics she spoke her native language with her pals, but mostly they kept their promises to help each other improve their English.

"Hi, Michael!" She ran to her friend and hugged him.

"Michael's hugging a girl!" one of the other boys groaned.

"Michael slugged Mai's shoulder gently. "Want to play ball?"

"Sure!" She gave him a little shove. "Anid I'll win!"

The gang ran to the ball diamond toting their bats and gloves, and a clumsy game of ball began.

"You swing like a girl, MaiLy!" Michael's teen-aged brother teased.

He came and stood behind her, showing her where to place her feet and how to hold the bat. After a couple practice swings, the first pitch was thrown. Mai smacked it near second base and yelled, "But I hit like boy!"

She ran to first base, still carrying the bat. Fortunately, Michael was playing second and was no better ball player than she. "Safe!" someone hollered and all members of both teams cheered. Just then a grown-up called that lunch was ready and they all headed toward the picnic tables.

Michael's brother put his arm around Mai's shoulder. "Now we just have to teach you to love Mom and apple pie."

"I love Mom," Mai grinned. "Show me apple pie."

After lunch, Connie tapped her spoon on a glass to get everyone's attention. She shared the plan for a new direction for FVNC. With the fall of Vietnam, they could no longer work there, so they were changing their name to Friends For Children—FFC-- and planning to expand their program into other countries. Everyone applauded and offered cheers of support for her and her staff.

"Without you we all wouldn't be here!" one mom called out.

After the homemade ice cream was cranked by all and served, Thuy gathered the children and joined them in singing Vietnamese songs. Mai and Michael sat arm in arm, smiling and rocking back and forth. Mai's eyes filled with tears when they began singing her favorite hymn. She hadn't heard that song or sung it since she huddled in the convent her last night at Domani de Marie. Michael must have noticed her smile disappear because he hugged her arm tighter as they sang the second verse.

Photographs of the airlift and magazine and newspaper articles about it were strewn across a tabletop. Dozens of children pored over them. Some started to cry as they pointed to things they recognized, while others chattered happily. Both emotions wrestled inside MaiLy as she traced her journey through the pictures.

Then Connie and Thuy gathered the adopted children under a shade tree. Thuy told them they could speak in either language as they talked about how they felt since the airlift. Some spoke of fear or frustration. Others shared feelings of loneliness and wondered where they fit in. When Mai was asked how she felt, she looked at Connie and said, "Happy." When she was prodded to speak of sadness, she refused. "Happy," she said again.

She silently hoped *if I don't think about it, maybe those other feelings will go away.*

CHAPTER 23

"Only ten days 'til school starts!" Marcie chimed. Mai frowned. "Don't be afraid. You'll do fine. You can do almost everything on the Kid's Page now and you do real good in all the workbooks Mom and Dad gave you. And, like you said, arithmetic is easy for you because adding is the same in any language."

"I learn much this summer," Mai said to bolster her own confidence.

"Besides, Mom says you'll be in fourth grade again 'til we see how you do," Marcie reassured her. "The best part about starting school is getting new clothes. We get to go to Target this afternoon and get three new outfits each!"

Connie came home from work late morning and announced they would go to lunch - - just the girls- - before shopping. They all put on dresses. Mai hadn't been able to figure yet if dresses were worn rarely because they were so special, or because women didn't like them much. Either way, it was fun to look dressed up at the nice restaurant.

They walked around the mall awhile, admiring the pretty clothes, then stopped at a shoe store where Mai,

Marcie, and Erica each got a pair of tennis shoes and "good" shoes. Marcie insisted on wearing her patent leather ones out of the store, but Mai wanted to keep hers looking new as long as possible, like her sandals in Vietnam.

Next they went to Target where Connie and the clerk patiently helped Mai locate every size eight dress in the store. The girls took turns zipping each other up and twirling in front of the mirrors. After nearly two hours, Connie suggested they make their final selections. They each eventually chose one dress, a pair of jeans, a new shirt, and shorts with a matching top. Just when Mai thought it didn't get any better than this, Connie took them to pick out six new pairs of socks and underwear.

The night before school started was spent deciding which outfit to wear with which coordinating socks. Mai thought Marcie looked as nervous and excited as she felt. Next they packed their backpacks with school supplies. Mai had never imagined the variety until they went to that department at Target. She stood in awe of the shelves loaded with pens, markers, crayons, and backpacks. She finally chose a Cinderella notebook and matching pencil case. When Connie bought her an entire ream of notebook paper, Mai told them about being punished for wasting one sheet to catch a bug at the orphanage.

She wondered if they believed her occasional stories and vowed to remember to keep them to herself.

It was hard to get to sleep that night, and Mai lay awake in the morning long before Pete called up the stairs to wake them.

She and Marcie walked hand in hand to the school building. Mai said she could find her classroom by herself, but was glad when her sister insisted on seeing her to the door.

"Hi, Mrs. Lawton!" Mai beamed.

"Hello, MaiLy! It is so good to see you again this year."

"I can read gooder now," Mai boasted. "I speak English!"

"Indeed you do," Mrs. Lawton smiled. "We'll have a great year together."

Mai hoped she was right.

As her classmates filed into the room, Mai was happy to see she knew many of them from the swimming pool crowd.

"Yo, MaiLy," Jason, one of the ornery boys, roared, raising his hand. "Gimme five!"

"Why you need five?" Mai asked, then blushed as the other boys laughed and slapped each other's palms in the air.

"Never mind them." It was her new friend Jenny from the pool. "Boys are a pain."

"They are painful?" Mai asked.

"You could say so. Come sit by me until Mrs. Lawton makes seat assignments."

They took desks near the window just as the bell rang. Mrs. Lawton welcomed everyone and seemed happy to see them. She asked the students to stand and say their names. Then she reviewed school and classroom rules. No running. No gum chewing. No talking out loud in class. Mai smiled as the rest of the rules were recited. She wondered what the nuns at Domani de Marie would think about needing these rules at all.

Sure enough, Jenny had been right. Next came seat assignments. The kids wandered around the classroom talking too loudly as they found their desks. Mai couldn't believe it when Jason slid into the one next to hers. She raised her hand and said, "Give five to me!"

Jason's smile covered his face as he slapped the palm of her hand.

"Mai, we got another call from the school today," Connie said as they cleared dishes from the supper table.

125

There was a family rule to not talk about problems during meal times, which was always a relief. But right after supper, when they were all together doing dishes, seemed to be a prime time to "deal with issues." That's why Mai always tried to get her chore done quickly and leave the room. Unfortunately, she hadn't been quick enough today.

"There have been only three months of school and this is the fourth time Mrs. Lawton has called saying you spend too much time talking in class. And when you aren't talking, you're daydreaming."

"I talk only when friends talk to me," Mai said, hoping that would end the discussion. But she knew better.

"I'm glad you have so many friends now, but if you talk to all of them, you're talking all the time. It's good that you made friends with Jason, but he is a -- a busy boy. You can't let him get you into trouble."

"Jason no get me trouble. I get trouble myself." Somehow, her argument didn't sound as good as when she'd rehearsed it. She figured her teacher was going to call again. At first the lack of strict discipline in the classroom had bothered Mai. But now, she had to admit, she was enjoying behaving the way most of the other kids did. She just hoped Mrs. Lawton hadn't mentioned the fight to her parents.

"What's this about a fight on the playground?" Connie persisted as she wiped the counters.

"No fight," Mai said.

"Mrs. Lawton said you were fighting."

"I only push boy who laugh at my English. He push back, so I push harder."

"That's not a good way to handle it, MaiLy. I know it's hard when they tease you, but you can't be getting into fights."

Mai clanged the dishes into the dishwasher and set her chin firmly. After a few minutes Connie said, "Mrs. Lawton says you don't pay attention in class - -that you seem to be daydreaming out the window." She tossed the sponge into the sink, sat on a chair, and pulled Mai into her arms. "Are you a daydreamer?" she asked, kissing Mai's head.

"Sister Katrine say I daydream too much."

"You miss Sister Katrine, don't you?"

"No. I happy here."

"I know you're happy here, Honey. But that doesn't mean you don't miss everyone you loved in Vietnam."

Mai stood silently in Connie's embrace.

"What do you daydream about?" Connie whispered. Mai hesitated.

"My mother in Vietnam," she breathed.

"It must be hard," Connie said, stroking Mai's hair, "knowing your mother brought you to the orphanage as a baby and left you there. She must have loved you very much to have given you to the nuns when she couldn't care for you. And it must be hard for you, not knowing who she was or what she looked like."

Mai pushed back gently, "I know her. I see her. And my brother and my sister."

"No, Honey. You had no family in Vietnam, remember? Only the nuns cared for you."

"No. I go to house of my mother. She take care of me."

"That's just a part of your daydream, MaiLy," Connie said, holding her close again. "It's normal for adopted kids to imagine their parents. Sometimes it's hard to know the difference between what is real and what is make believe, isn't it?"

"Yes," Mai conceded, rocking in Connie's arms.

CHAPTER 24

Mai hated the weekly family meetings. Hate was a forbidden word in the house, so she corrected her thought to *really, really, disliking them.* It was supposed to be a time of sharing ideas, problems, and information. During her two years in the family, she had, however, learned to play the family meeting game. It took her a long time to realize that things went much better if she said what her parents wanted to hear instead of what she was really thinking or feeling.

That approach, worked at the group sharing session at FVNC gatherings too. Connie, being a social worker and the program director, usually led them. She spent a lot of time trying to get the adoptees to grieve their loss of country and culture. Mai was glad to see so many of her friends open up and share their deepest feelings, which Connie often helped them identify. But Mai could never seem to identify her own, in spite of persistent coaxing. She finally decided it was a lot easier to just agree with whatever feelings Connie suggested.

Her folks seemed especially excited about tonight's family meeting. They hustled everyone through the kitchen duties after supper and left pots and pans soaking in the sink, a rare exception to a strict rule. The meeting began with announcing changes in the chore list. Since Mai was almost twelve now, she would be responsible for cleaning the living room and dining room. Marcie, at age nine, would see to it that the bathrooms were clean every morning. Even though Erica was only seven, she was old enough to take on more responsibility. She would keep the playroom in order since most of it was her junk anyway.

They moved through the problem-sharing part of the meeting rather quickly since Mai, of course, denied any problems. Marcie asked that everyone try not to make such a mess in the bathroom since it was her chore now and Erica simply wanted to go on record as saying it wasn't always her mess in the play room.

Finally their parents got to the information part of the meeting and nearly burst when they announced the plan to adopt a brother and sister from Korea. All three girls squealed and ran to see the photos Connie and Pete held. They had discussed this possibility at other family meetings and it had been generally agreed that their family was so wonderful they would have lots to offer another child. But, two?

"Are they twins?" Marcie gasped.

"No, they're brother and sister, though. He's six and she's five," Pete said pointing to the black children in the photo.

"So, I'll still be bigger," Erica said with relief.

Glad to no longer be the only adopted child in the family, Mai asked, "How soon will they come?"

"We don't know for sure," Connie said. "Maybe in a few weeks."

"What will we name them?" Erica piped up.

Pete chuckled. "They already have names. David and Sara."

The girls agreed those were good names and repeated them a few times to make sure.

LeAnn Thieman

The remainder of the meeting was spent making arrangements for their arrival. The guest bedroom would be made into their room for now, but eventually Sara would share a room with Erica and David would have a room of his own.

"They'll want to be together for a while," Connie said.

"Sure," Mai offered. "It's scary coming to a new country and a new family. At least they'll have each other."

Marcie was prepared to post signs labeling all the household objects until Connie said they already knew English. They had been raised in an American sponsored orphanage in Korea. No, she didn't know how long they had been there.

The meeting was adjourned with their usual family group-hug.

It took two months for the big day to finally arrive. Everyone had played a part in getting the house ready for the newest family members and together they made a banner welcoming them. Erica even took the empty fast food sacks and miscellaneous toys out of the station wagon before they headed to the airport through the January snow.

They waited anxiously as the plane taxied to the gate. Connie teased Pete that he was pacing like an expectant father.

Hundreds of passengers walked by until the exit ramp was deserted. The three girls glared at their mom, pleading for an explanation.

"Be patient," Connie said. "They're coming."

Just then a flight attendant walked slowly toward them with a child clinging to each of her arms. They both looked much smaller than in the photos taped to the front of the refrigerator. He wore faded black pants that barely touched the tops of his ankles, revealing socks that didn't match. His hair was shaved close to his head and his eyes looked as worried as his sister's. Barrettes held her short, bushy black hair back from her frowning face. Her dress was at least one size too big, and looked like it had been worn by many little

130

girls before her. Connie and Pete approached them and squatted to their level.

"Hello, David. Hello Sara. We are so happy to see you," Connie said softly.

The youngsters held each other's hands and took a few steps forward.

"Pleased to meet you," they said in unison, then bowed slightly. David extended his hand to Pete, who took his son's hand and shook it gently. Connie motioned for the girls to come closer then spread her arms. "This is your family."

"I know," David said, his bright smile erasing the worry. He reached into the pocket of his shirt and pulled out a crumpled picture of them, sent to him months ago. Poking at the photo, he said, "Mai, Marcie, Erica." As he did so, each of the girls bounced in place. "Now I have FOUR sisters!"

"And we finally have a brother!" Marcie said.

"And another sister," Mai said, patting Sara's woolly head.

Sara smiled shyly. The flight attendant handed Pete a small duffel bag, explaining that it was all they'd brought with them.

"Let's go home, family!" Pete proclaimed, leading the procession as they all traipsed through the terminal, cleaving to each other.

Mai and Marcie doted on David and Sara and had to be reminded not to treat them like toddlers. Erica was indifferent, as she had been when Mai came, and declined to join in tutoring David in second grade and Sara in first. Mai was glad the family attention shifted to the new members and away from her.

Things went generally well for the months to come. Mai took classes to improve her English, so there were fewer worrisome phone calls from school. She excelled in gymnastics, loved ballet, and began tennis lessons in the spring. Her essay entitled *My Family* won not only a state contest, but also the loving praise of her parents. Mai's favorite after school activity, however, was babysitting classes. Her certificate of completion took a place of honor on the refrigerator door and Mai gloated when the Smith family next door claimed she was the best sitter they'd ever had. "Babysitting reminds me of the little kids at the orphanage," Mai confided to Marcie one day. "I miss them sometimes."

Connie's work with FVNC increased as the organization expanded to other countries, so the already organized household routines became even more structured. Once a month, the entire family went to the supermarket and left wheeling three carts full of food. Every Sunday after church, the afternoon was spent preparing and freezing meals for the following week. Even school lunches were frozen as much as possible to save time packing them on busy mornings. Everyone had a task in this assembly line production, which, for the most part, was fun family time. Even Sara was assigned to grate cheese or label packaged meals. Her penmanship provided lots of jokes and "mystery suppers."

"We're a family and we all work together," Pete would say as he opened a twenty-pound package of hamburger or stirred a double batch of batter.

Sundays were still the mandatory family meeting days, too. One Sunday, nearly a year and a half after David and Sara's arrival, Connie had been particularly successful in getting them to talk about their feelings about leaving Korea. When David talked about missing his birth mother, Connie listened attentively and reaffirmed his feelings of loss.

Mai squirmed in her chair, but said nothing.

When Connie asked Sara if she felt the same way, she simply shrugged. Connie gently coaxed her to talk about how sad it must feel to leave her homeland and family.

"Stop telling her what to think!" Mai found herself shouting. The rest of the family just stared at her, looking as surprised and confused as she felt. Mai had no idea what had prompted her to speak up that way, but there was no sense in stopping now. "You always try to tell us how to feel!" she bellowed.

"I'm not trying to tell anyone how to feel, MaiLy," Connie answered with a firm voice. "I'm just trying to help each of you figure that out."

"Maybe we don't know!" Mai had never yelled this way and it frightened her that she couldn't stop. "Why do you believe him when he talks about missing his mother and you won't believe me when I say that?"

"Because, MaiLy," Connie answered calmly, "David and Sara remember their mother. They lived with her until they were three and five…"

"I remember my mother!"

"MaiLy." Connie walked to Mai and tried to hug her but Mai slapped her arm away hard.

"MaiLy!" Pete reprimanded. "Do not hit your mom!"

Mai had never heard his voice so stern. "She's not my mom!" Mai felt her face bursting red with anger.

Connie backed away. "Honey, I AM your mom," she said softly. "I'm the only mom you've ever known. I know it feels better to imagine your birth mother as being real, but that's only a daydream. The orphanage reports say your mother left you on the doorstep there when you were a tiny baby…"

"Don't start about how she loved me so much she gave me away!"

Pete spoke up in a kinder voice this time. "But that's true, Mai. That's the greatest love there is…"

"Well, you say you love us so much." She motioned to Sara and David who were starting to cry, "So what's to say you won't give us away!"

Connie and Pete stared at each other with no response. Then Pete said, "We will NEVER give you away. There is nothing you could ever do that will make us love you less. And nothing that will ever make us give you away."

"Oh, yeah?" Mai challenged.

As she stormed out the back door she heard Erica cry, "I'm so sick of the adopted kids getting all the attention. Why doesn't anyone care as much about how I feel? I'm sorry I voted for all this in the first place..."

Mai wanted to run and keep running but didn't know where to go.

It's hard to know where to run when you don't know where you belong.

She plopped between rows of corn in the garden, wrapped her arms around herself, and tried not to cry. The shadow of the corn stalks shielded her. She slipped off her shoes and felt the cool, damp soil between her toes and smelled the sweet scent of strawberries.

"I should have stayed in Vietnam." She had never allowed that thought to surface in her mind, let alone be spoken. She hugged her knees and rested her head on them.

Thunder rumbled and raindrops rustled the corn leaves and trickled off, mixing with her tears. She walked around the house over and over again as if the drenching rain could wash away the loneliness. Finally she settled on the front porch swing, shivering from both anger and cold. The conversation inside had gone from everybody yelling, to all of them talking in softer voices. For a second she almost felt sorry for what she'd done - - for Connie - - she tried hard to help people figure out what's inside them. But any sympathy Mai felt was immediately dashed by anger, rumbling like the thunder inside her. *She doesn't hear me. She doesn't believe me. She never will.*

The swing's rhythmic squeaking and the pattering of the rain soothed her. It seemed like hours passed before the murmur of the family meeting finished. Mai wondered if it ended in a group hug this time.

Pete surprised her when he came out the front door and sat beside her. She wiped her face with the back of her hand

and scooted to the opposite end of the swing, facing away from him.

"Remember when we used to swing together in Vietnam?" he asked softly. "You'd sit on my lap and we'd hug each other."

Mai nodded, staring into the rain as if it held answers.

"I photographed those moments in my mind. Those are some of my favorite memories."

Had he captured them the same way she had? They were some of her most beloved daydreams.

"I suppose now that you're thirteen you're a bit too big for that, huh?"

Mai bit the inside of her lip to stifle a smile.

Then, though she hadn't planned on saying it, she blurted, "Why did you pick ME, Dad?"

The swing creaked a few more times. "You picked me, remember?"

She turned to face him. His eyes were red. Had he been crying? She wanted to throw her arms around him and sway like they did in their memories. But instead she turned again to the rain.

"I'm not sure Mom would have picked me." They chuckled together for only a second, then sat in silence again.

"There's something she doesn't like about me."

"She loves you, Mai," he answered tenderly.

"Seems like I can't do anything right by her. You both said I was in charge after school. I called Mom every day when we got home, at exactly four o'clock. If I were ten minutes late, she'd get mad at me. And I'm supposed to make sure the house is clean when you guys get home. But when I tell the kids to pick up their junk, they tell her I'm bossy and she believes them and yells at me. She never believes me."

"It's hard being the oldest," he conceded. "We're just trying to teach you responsibility. If it feels like we're hard on you, I'm sorry."

She stared into his tormented face. "No. I'm sorry, Dad."

As he reached across the swing and stroked her arm, she slid into his embrace.

She felt him kiss the top of her damp head. "We love you, MaiLy," he whispered.

"I love you too." She rested her head on his shoulder. The thunderstorm subsided. Taking a deep breath, Mai felt the fresh air cleanse the anger polluting her heart. She smiled faintly when she noticed a rainbow forming in the clearing sky.

CHAPTER 25

"Were just trying to teach you responsibility." His words ricocheted in her head a million times over the next few years. They echoed as she did most of the laundry, then was scolded for shrinking and fading it. When the other kids didn't do the work on their daily chore card, Mai reminded them repeatedly, only to be reprimanded for nagging. Connie was gone overseas periodically and Mai took responsibility for the housework while she was away. Connie always seemed genuinely appreciative, then. She praised Mai and usually brought her a special gift. It made Mai wish she'd be gone more often. But, in no time, the friction between them resurfaced. It seemed no matter how hard she tried, she couldn't please her mother - - she couldn't please anyone.

Eventually she stopped trying.

Responsibility. Either she had too much or not enough. When they told her how to catch the city bus to gymnastics, when she'd only been in the country a year, it seemed like too much. When she missed that bus, she cried so hard a nice lady stopped and took her home with her. After feeding her cookies and milk, the woman finally reached Connie to come retrieve her daughter. Her Mom had been furious, warning Mai about dangers in the city. *I know about dangerous cities,* Mai thought. *Nha Trang was a dangerous city.*

If they're so big on responsibility, Mai often wondered, *why won't they let me be responsible for picking my own friends?* Her folks considered many of her freshman class friends to be "losers" and wouldn't let her spend time at their homes. She went anyway, knowing she'd be grounded when she did.

She abandoned the childish recreation of roller-skating and refused to ride her out-dated three-speed bicycle. The only bikes on the rack at high school were ten speeds. As if trying to satisfy a craving she couldn't identify, she began eating too much, too often. Her chubby figure caused her to dislike herself even more. Resentment grew when Connie reminded her every morning to exercise with Richard Simmons on TV.

There were happy times, but those seemed too infrequent, mostly because Mai refused to join in. When the younger girls braided Pete's hair, painted tattoos on his arms, or gave him back rubs, she longed to be in on that fun again. But she refused to allow herself that little girl glee. Summer camping expeditions were still fun - - the sing-alongs in the car; marshmallow roasts and ghost stories over the campfire; and long hikes with the whole troupe wearing matching shirts with whistles attached. But because it was a natural time for reflection, "dealing with issues and feelings often spoiled it

The Denver Bronco party had been fun. Pete was always a fan, but last year he'd taken his enthusiasm to a new level. Everyone in the family found something orange to wear while they watched the game, waving orange pompoms and blowing horns. They drank orange pop and ate orange chips and dip served in a bowl shaped like a

Denver Bronco helmet. Pete huddled the family members to explain the basics of the game.

"Okay, Mai. You're quarterback John Elway," he said dragging her from the couch and shoving her into the middle of the living room. Mai pretended to be annoyed as he sent David to the other end of the room to be her wide receiver. Connie and the girls applauded and cheered as Pete introduced himself as a Pro-Bowl defensive end. When he tackled Mai to the carpet, they rolled around and laughed like old times. That afternoon the tension between them seemed to be blocked, tackled, and contained too. But Mai's defiant behavior afterward resulted in a penalty. As she sulked in her room, she wondered why she reacted the way she did- - why she spoiled everything.

One of the few things that made her happy was baby-sitting. The little Smith boys were six and eight now, and loved her no matter how much trouble she was in. Mai wished she could interact with her own brother and sisters as well as she did with Luke and Timmy, but it seemed too late for that. They'd had too many quarrels.

When Mai got a D minus in history, she knew it wouldn't go unpunished. Why would any kid take that report card home to her parents? Mai expected to be grounded for at least a week, so she figured she might as well earn the punishment big-time. Throwing her report card in the ditch, she went to a home her parents prohibited. Shelly's folks weren't nearly as strict as Mai's and wouldn't care who stayed there or for how long.

"But, just to be safe," Shelly cautioned, "you'd better hide in the closet until the coast is clear."

The coast didn't clear for two days.

Shelly smuggled food to her stowaway friend, who sat wedged atop the shoe rack most of that time. On the third day, Mai changed into some of Shelly's clothes, which fit poorly on her increasingly chubby body, and headed to school, exhausted and achy. Her friends buzzed about frantic calls they'd gotten from Connie and Pete, but agreed that parents deserved to be shaken up once in awhile. Guilt tore at Mai's insides until she went home sick mid-morning. The shame intensified when she found her parents pacing the floor, staring at the phone. She felt she deserved any discipline doled out, but after thirty days of marching to her room after school and completing four extra credit reports for history, she changed her mind about the fairness of that punishment.

A few months later, her parents surprised her with a new ten-speed bike for her sixteenth birthday. Instinctively, she threw her arms around them. She lingered there and silently vowed never to run away or hurt them again.

She broke her promise twice in the months to come.

Mai knew her parents were right about Anita—she wasn't a good influence. Anita's parents didn't seem to care what she did, where she went, or how late she stayed. Mai thought that seemed to be an ideal living situation and couldn't figure why it didn't make Anita happier. Mai sneaked out of the house as often as she could to enjoy the freedom at Anita's house. Her new friend taught her to smoke cigarettes, which was no easy task. It took days of relentless coughing, choking and vomiting to convince her body the habit was "cool." Before going home, always deliberately late, Mai chewed gum and washed off heavy black eye make-up. She made it a practice to ignore her parents' prodding questions and push past them, slamming the door of her room behind her. When Marcie tried to talk to her there, she repeated her usual explanation for her behavior. "You wouldn't understand."

On a nippy fall morning, Mai rode her new bike to the grocery store with Anita to buy pop and cigarettes. Her legs grew tired and she panted trying to keep up. Her denim jacket had barely snapped around her this morning. She hated her fat body. Pete and Connie reminded her often that she wasn't really "fat" and, besides, outer appearances didn't matter so much. They assured her that it's what's on the inside of a person that counts.

"I hate my outside and my inside!" Mai wheezed, peddling behind her friend. They locked their bikes on the rack at the grocery store where her family shopped every week. Mai ignored friendly glances and greetings from familiar clerks, and strutted to the cosmetics aisle while Anita went for pop. As she debated between jet-black and black mascara, her eyes caught the diet pill sign. Lose fifteen pounds in just four weeks. Mai picked up a package and read the details. Become a new you. Increase your self-esteem.

Mai looked nonchalantly to the left, then to the right - - then slipped the box of pills into the front of her jacket. She glanced both ways again, her heart hammering. She grabbed three more packages, jammed them past the snaps, and hustled to find Anita at the check out counter.

"You gonna pay for those?" the clerk asked.

"Just did," Anita said slamming her money onto the counter.

"No, I'm talking to your friend," the clerk barked.

Mai felt someone grip her shoulder. "You'd better come with me," said the man behind her.

"Bug off!" Mai answered, jerking away.

"Store security." He grabbed her arm.

"No!" Mai rammed her shoulder into him. He stumbled back against the candy bar display, sending Snickers and Butterfingers sailing. Lunging toward her, he grabbed her jacket, tearing it open. The diet pills fell to the floor as she struggled to pull away from his hold. The male checker seized one arm while the security guard grabbed the other.

"Like I said. You'd better come with me."

Shoppers stared as the two men forcefully escorted Mai to the manager's office.

Anita was nowhere in sight.

Mai fell into the chair and folded her arms. She refused to give her name until a familiar clerk came into the room to identify her. "MaiLy, what are you doing?" the woman pleaded before she was instructed to leave the room again.

"Don't bother to call my mom and dad. They're out of town," Mai lied. "Just let me go for now and when they get back next week we'll straighten all this out." She got to her feet, but the guard gently nudged her back into her chair.

The phone number she finally gave the security guard could not be completed as dialed. Mai sneered when the manager had to resort to looking it up in the phone book.

Ten minutes later, Connie stormed into the room screaming. "What on earth do you think you're doing!"?

"What I do is none of your business." Mai blinked back tears, hoping her hateful glare would keep them from forming.

"It is my business when the police are involved!"

Mai's expression turned to one of fear.

Connie turned to the manager. "You WILL be filing a police report, won't you?"

"That's optional on my part," he answered.

"File it!" Connie snapped.

Mai's face blanched.

"Now is there anything you want to say to my daughter before I take her home?"

The manager looked at Mai sadly from behind his desk. "Just that you are no longer welcome in this store, MaiLy." Then with a nod from Connie he took a Polaroid camera from the drawer. "It's policy to take your picture so employees will recognize you should you try to return."

The flash in her face made Mai feel like the felon she was. She deserved to have a mug shot taken.

The silent car ride home was more painful than any words could have been. But the pain in her father's eyes when she walked into the house increased her own a hundred fold.

"What is wrong with you?" The question was fair enough, but Mai just didn't have an answer. More questions came firing. "How many times have you stolen before?"

"Never!"

"I don't believe you!"

"You never believe me!"

"How can we?" Pete slammed his fist on the hall table. "You're a liar! And, now, apparently, a thief!"

"You'll never understand!" Mai yelled so loudly it hurt her throat. "I should have stayed in Vietnam!" She pounded up the stairs two at a time.

She lay sobbing into her pillow, mourning their question - - her question. *What is wrong with me?*

CHAPTER 26

Mai's second year in high school was no easier than her first.

Poor report cards meant more family fights. Grounding became a way of life. Mai used her babysitting money to buy tight stretch pants, heavy make-up, and mousse to spike her hair straight up in front. When Pete or Connie criticized her look, she responded with, "You're just trying to make me into a preppie!"

During one heated argument, Connie yelled, "You look like a slut!"

Pete, who rarely became involved in these discussions, or any other discipline for that matter, said, "Boys will misunderstand, MaiLy, if you dress that way."

She shot back, "You say it doesn't matter how you look on the outside, it's what's on the inside that counts!"

But that philosophy didn't seem to apply in this case.

Mai was bewildered by their interpretation of her dress, because she'd always been a very modest person. She was never comfortable undressing in front of other girls in P.E. class, and not even in front of her sisters at home.

But she wouldn't give her folks the satisfaction of knowing she was not at all interested in sex and, to be honest, was afraid of it. Early on, Connie had taught her that having sex and making love were not necessarily the same thing. She had stressed that intercourse was a beautiful act of supreme love to be shared only with the person you marry. Mai agreed that sounded beautiful, and was not eager to consider it until then. If she had shared her attitude about this with her folks, they probably would not have gone ballistic when they found her friend Ryan in her bedroom last month. Pete discovered him there with his shirt off. It was the first time he ever struck MaiLy.

"Get the hell out of my house!" he screamed to the boy. When Mai opened her mouth in protest, Pete slapped her face. They stared at each other, both their eyes filled with pain. Then Pete stormed out of the room.

The incident was never mentioned again.

Luke and Timmy didn't care what she looked like, and loved her unconditionally. Baby-sitting for them was one of the few things she did right - - until the spring of that year.

She had gotten the two youngsters ready for bed, and snuggled with them in their Ninja Turtle pajamas to read them stories. They were having a bedtime snack in the kitchen when a knock came at the back door. Mai slid her chair back from the table and walked the few steps to the door. She unlocked it but left the chain in place as she peeked through the three-inch opening. "Who is it?"

"I'm looking for Mr. Smith," the man said. "I'm a friend of his."

"He's not home," Mai answered politely.

"When do you expect him?"

"Not for another hour," she said, closing the door and locking it again. She heard his muffled "thanks anyway" as he walked away.

Before the ice cream bowls were empty, a knock came again.

Mai opened the door with the chain still in place. It splintered and flung open as the forceful kick knocked her to the floor. The same man lurked above her with a ten-inch knife in his fist. His stringy brown hair draped the collar of his worn, plaid shirt. A smirk sneered across his unshaven face, showing crooked teeth that seemed to get in the way when he droned, "You shoulda let me in."

"What do you want?" MaiLy panted, as she got to her feet and rushed to the whimpering boys. With trembling hands, she drew them to her.

"You know what I want," he growled. Then waving his knife, he said, "Get on in the back room."

Slowly Mai walked to the bedroom with Luke and Timmy sobbing and clinging to her side. "I'll protect you," she promised, knowing she would be powerless to do so. She stopped at the bedroom door, but his shove hurled them into the middle of the room.

"Take your clothes off!" he barked. "All of you!"

"Don't hurt the boys." Mai pleaded past tears caught in her throat. "I'll do whatever you want, but please don't hurt the little boys."

"Take your clothes off!" His angry eyes narrowed as he screamed the command and waved the knife at them.

Only when Mai started to unbutton her blouse did Luke and Timmy fumble with the buttons on their pajamas.

"Now!" their enemy bellowed. The boys jumped with fear then stumbled out of their clothes and stood in their under shorts, shaking and crying louder.

Mai stood immobilized by fear, confusion, and shame. Her breathing pounded as rapidly as her heart. He stepped toward her and put his face within inches of hers. His rotten breath seeped between his twisted teeth. "Now!" he hissed as he dragged the icy blade across her cheek.

She slipped her blouse slowly off her shoulders and it fell to the floor.

Then his powerful grip seized a fistful of her hair. Her scalp and forehead stretched and burned beneath his grasp.

146

With a blow to the top of her head, he slammed her to her knees in front of him. With the weapon still in his hand, he unzipped his grungy blue jeans and they dropped to his ankles. From the corner of her eye, Mai saw Luke and Timmy, their heads buried in each other's embrace. Succumbing to her terror, she cried out, "Run, Luke and Timmy, run!"

Her assailant yanked her head back and grazed the knife against her throat while the boys raced out of the room.

Then, he stripped Mai of her clothing, her innocence, and remaining self-esteem.

The faded cry of the police siren grew louder. For an instant, Mai hoped she would be rescued- -but then knew it was too late- - this suffering would never end. Her assailant zipped up his jeans, as she lay slumped on the floor. Mai expected he would kill her -- and was disappointed he didn't before he fled.

Dr. Henry had been her pediatrician and a friend since Mai first arrived in Denver. There was no kinder, gentler man. Yet his exam this night seemed like a continuation of the assault. At the police station, Connie softly encouraged Mai to "cooperate" as she looked through pages and pages of mug shots. Finally back home, her parents' tender hugs, and "I'm so sorry this happened" did little to ease her pain.

She lay in a fetal curl wondering if she would spend the rest of her life crying herself to sleep.

CHAPTER 27

Mai slammed the door as hard as she could, hoping the beveled glass would break. "I'm running away for good this time! You'll never see me again!" she screamed, smearing tears from her cheeks.

"I'll show them," she panted. "I ran before and I can run again!"

So she ran for hours, wondering how she had gotten to this place in her life and where she was going from here. Her sobs echoed in the hollow emptiness inside her as her bare feet beat the pavement.

Abandoned again.

She collapsed into a pile of leaves in the park and rested awhile. The crisp autumn air and scent of fallen leaves normally filled her with excitement and joy. But now that aroma, and the crunching beneath her, tore at her fearful heart.

By the time she got to Shelly's house, she had pounded through feelings of anger, hatred, and self-pity, to resignation. She deserved this.

Shelly opened the door. "MaiLy, what's wrong?" This was the first time Mai noticed that, though blonde, Shelly looked just like her -- same hair style, makeup, and clothes.

"They kicked me out!" Mai found her anger again.

"You're kidding!" Shelly said, closing the door behind them and flopping onto the couch. "I can't believe that. I didn't think they'd ever give up on you. Though I wouldn't blame them if they did, after all the trouble you've gotten into since last spring. What happened?" She motioned Mai to sit beside her on the leather sofa.

Mai heaved a sigh. It felt good to sit after running most of the afternoon. She brushed dirt from the bottom of her red, rough feet. But that pain didn't compare to the agony in her heart. "They said, 'If you're so unhappy here, then why don't you leave?'"

"My folks tried to pull that tough love crap on me last year. Don't worry. The guilt will get to them soon and they'll come crawling back, begging you to come home."

"I don't want to go home! I don't need them. I don't need anybody -- except maybe you. Can I crash here 'til I figure out what to do?"

"Sure. My folks are gone for a month and I'm on my own again. I have this huge place all to myself. Why they ever built this six bedroom mansion I'll never know." She lit a cigarette. "But, hey. What they do is their business." She took a long drag from her smoke and smiled, "And what I do is mine. You and I will have a blast, doing whatever we want, whenever we want."

That's just the freedom Mai yearned for.

So why did she feel so scared and sad?

"Have a smoke; you'll feel better," Shelly said, tossing a pack of cigarettes into her lap. "My folks left with beer still in the refrigerator. Now THAT will REALLY make you feel better."

Mai hesitated. She had sipped beer at a few parties, but mostly just held the can most of the night. Connie had warned that alcohol impairs a person's judgment and made girls do things they normally wouldn't do. Mai always figured she had a big enough problem with that already.

She followed Shelly to the kitchen and caught the beer can she tossed to her. Mai popped the top and clanked her can against Shelly's.

"To freedom!" Shelly cheered.

Mai swigged four gulps of the bitter drink. Her face puckered and she coughed, spewing the last mouthful down her shirt. She forced a laugh. "To happiness!" she added, guzzling the rest of the can.

Pete sat on the edge of the bed, his head cradled in his hands. "Where is she? It's been almost a week. She's never run away for this long before. Oh, I shouldn't have been so hard on her," he moaned.

Connie sat beside him. "We couldn't let her break the rules, and hold the other kids to them." She stared ahead blankly. "Maybe I gave her too much responsibility."

They held each other in silence, rocking on the edge of the bed.

"Maybe I was gone too much. I've been working so hard to become a full partner in the firm, maybe I wasn't here enough."

"You're a wonderful dad, Pete," Connie whispered. "It's not about you. It's not even about me. We knew going into this that older kids have a much harder time adjusting after adoption. Remember? We talked about this even before we decided to adopt. We said we'd risk it- -that it would be worth it- -for us and the child."

"I love her so much." Pete choked, then he cried out loud when he added, "She picked me!"

"I know," Connie soothed. "I love her, too. After working so hard to get her, it's hard to let her go. But, obviously, we can't make her stay."

"Maybe we should have gotten her more counseling - -especially after the assault."

"Pete, we tried two different counselors. Mai refused to talk to them or to us. What else could we do?" Connie stroked his head. "We can keep track of her through the other kids. We'll know if she's ever in real danger." She forced a smile. "We both know she was created to be our child. I still believe that. She'll be back."

Mai tried going to school to complete her senior year, but headaches and hangovers made concentration and studying even harder than before. The only positive part was seeing Marcie there. Her forgiving, and always loving, sister met her at her locker every morning and filled her in on family news.

Shelly's prediction that her parents would soon beg Mai to come home, was wrong. Marcie reiterated how much they said they loved her, but that she was not welcome back until she could "toe the line." Mai slammed her locker shut and winced as the sound crashed in her aching head.

"Come home, MaiLy," Marcie pleaded.

"I can't. I finally found the freedom I've been looking for all my life."

"I'm not sure this 'freedom' is good for you. You look awful."

"Thanks a lot." They shared a loving glance and smile. "I left without anything, and Shelly's clothes don't fit me so good. This is her mom's." Mai tugged at the long sleeved sweatshirt she was wearing.

Marcie persisted. "At least come home after school, before Mom and Dad get home. I can sneak you in so you can get your stuff." The class bell blasted as the plan was set.

Marcie went in the house first to make sure a parent hadn't come home early. "Coast is clear," she called from the porch.

Mai crept from behind a bush and into the house. A part of her wanted to hug the walls, the floor, and the banister; yet another part felt like a trespasser in her own home.

David and Sara ran to her, smothering her with hugs, kisses and questions. While she wadded her clothes into a duffel bag, they quizzed her about where she stayed and what she was doing. David followed her to the closet and held the hangers as she ripped clothes off them and jammed more into her bag.

"We miss you," he finally murmured.

Mai flopped onto the edge of her bed and David and Sara snuggled beside her. "I miss you, too."

"I can't figure out," he fixed his sad brown eyes on hers, "why, if a person waited their whole life to have a home, they would run away from it."

Mai sat staring at him, then shook her head slowly. "I can't figure it out either."

"Well look who's here," Erica sneered from the doorway. "Come home to make more trouble? Or just to steal more things?"

Marcie shot her a sour look.

"I'm not stealing. This is my stuff." Mai got up from the bed and grabbed her backpack.

"Hope that's how Mom sees it. She's pulling into the garage now," Erica threatened.

With one stroke of her arm, Mai swept every item from her dresser top into her backpack. Shoving her curling iron and hair dryer into her bag, she turned to her siblings.

"Gotta go." She ruffled David's hair with her hand, then stooped to receive his hug.

"Come back soon," Sara whimpered

Mai stood, flung the pack onto her back, then put both arms around Marcie. "Thanks, Sis. See ya around," she said softly.

When they heard the back door open, Mai bolted down the front stairs and fled with her life's possessions on her back.

A refugee again.

CHAPTER 28

The beer was no longer bitter. It washed away the loneliness. Shelly was right; if you drank enough of it, you did feel better. Swarms of their friends joined them every night in the sedating ritual.

It took months of practice for Mai to learn how much to drink to drown the pain without losing complete control. For reasons she couldn't explain, not stepping over that line was still important to her. When drunken partygoers stooped to lewd and sexual misbehaviors, Mai huddled alone in a corner, refusing vulgar offers to join in.

Drinking until dawn and sleeping until noon left little time for school. Mai dropped out second semester to devote full time to her freedom.

When Shelly's parents returned from their trip, they kicked Mai and their daughter out of their home. The girls stayed at various friends' homes for a few weeks, until Shelly's parents called, begging her to come home again. Then Mai started sleeping wherever the party was.

The park near her parents' home was a perfect place to meet David, Sara, or Marcie after school. That was about the same time of day Mai would wake up and sober up. She tried to clean up the best she could and put drops in her eyes and a fake smile on her face to convince them, and herself, that she was happy. Her efforts were futile.

"You look like crap!" Marcie said one spring afternoon. They spread their heavy jackets on the ground and lay gazing at the sapphire sky. The grass was turning green and tulips bloomed in the flowerbed beside them. "I can't believe you're happier now than when you were at home."

"I don't know where home is," Mai admitted. "Sometimes I really do think I'd have been better off staying in Vietnam. Wonder who I would be if I'd been raised by my birth mother."

"You'd probably be selling vegetables at a street stand." Marcie rolled onto her stomach and looked into her sister's face. "Or you'd be a prostitute. You know that's how lots of girls survived there."

Mai looked away and stared again at the cloudless sky.

Marcie continued softly, "But your birth mother was long gone, Mai. Why do you keep bringing her up?"

"I don't know. I really believe I remember her," Mai sighed. "But Mom's right. I am a daydreamer. I don't know what's real and what's not anymore."

A breeze fanned nearby trees, sprinkling cherry blossom petals around them.

"The orphanage was going to send me to France," Mai chuckled. "Just think; I could've been a nun!"

Giggles turned to laughter when Marcie crooned, "Sister Mary MaiLy!"

Mai's smile faded. "Maybe I'd have been better off there." She draped her arm over her face and mumbled. "I thought I was a good person. How'd I ever get this bad?"

"You're not bad," Marcie soothed, patting her sister's shoulder.

"Oh, yeah? Just ask Mom and Dad. There's no sense in my trying to be good when they're convinced I'm bad."

"They love you, Mai. You have no idea how hard it is for them to let you go like this. I hear them talking sometimes. More than anything, they want to bring you home again, but they know it wouldn't work; you wouldn't stay." Marcie paused. "I heard Dad say it's all he can do to keep from rescuing you again."

They lay sprawled on the grass in silence and breathed in the fresh spring air. Watching robins playing tug-of-war with a worm brought another round of giggles.

Mai finally sighed, "I gotta figure out where I belong."

Her sister said nothing, but reached over and held Mai's hand.

A few minutes later, Marcie got up and brushed grass from the back of her jeans and headed for home. Mai lay awhile longer, enveloped in loneliness.

Suddenly a football bounced next to her head, startling her to a sitting position.

"Sorry."

Mai shielded her eyes from the sun to see a handsome young man standing over her. She picked up the ball and got to her feet. He was a few inches taller than Mai, and had broad shoulders and muscular arms.

"Guess I'm not a very good catch," he said, reaching for the ball.

"No problem," Mai was so transfixed by his deep brown eyes; she forgot to let go of the ball. As he tugged it gently from her hands, it was her turn to say, "Sorry."

His long, sandy -brown hair was parted in the middle and touched the collar of his faded denim shirt.

"Hey, Ray!" his friends hollered. "You gonna play ball or pick up chicks?"

"Don't pay any attention to them," he stammered, staring at the ground. "They got no manners." Then his penetrating brown eyes met Mai's again. She thought she saw there the sorrow and loneliness reflected in her own.

"I'm MaiLy," she said, blushing.

"Ray Martinez. You live around here?"

"I used to. My folks kicked me out, so now I live all over."

"Hey, Lover-boy!" his buddies bellowed.

"Better go. Will you be here tomorrow?" he asked shyly.

"Maybe."

"Try," he said, and jogged back to his teammates.

Mai met Ray in the park the next day and the day after that. Their first meetings were awkward; each of them obviously hoping the other would lead the conversation. But soon they learned they had too much in common.

"I've had a rough life," Ray lamented as they sat together on top of a picnic table. "Lots of it I'm not proud of. Stole some stuff a few years back."

"Me too," Mai said to his obvious disbelief.

"Spent some time in Juvenile Hall. Ran away from there. And my folks didn't give a damn. Seems like I can't do nothin' right by them."

"I know the feeling."

"I got to move out of there, but I don't know where to go."

"Why do you think I live wherever the party is? I've got no place to go either."

"Speaking of parties. We're throwing a ragin' one tonight," Ray grinned. "Want to come?"

They went to a party that night and the night after that. Their conversations started to flow as freely as the booze. Mai told him about her life in Vietnam and adoption here. When she tried to explain where it all went wrong, she had to admit she still didn't have a clue.

"But you had a Dad, a family who really wanted you," Ray protested. "I ain't never felt that. I may still be livin' with my folks, but it feels like they gave me up same as your mom in Vietnam gave you up."

"No, if they're your real mom and dad, stay with them," Mai said confidently. "You can work things out."

"You're somethin', you know that?"

Mai just shrugged.

Ray put his arms around her and drew her close. "With all the problems you got, you're still trying to help me." He kissed her for the first time. "I shouldn't fall in love with you. I got more problems than you know."

Whoops and hollers came from the adjoining room. Mai could see Shelly undressing in front of the crowd and knew what would happen next.

"Let's get out of here," Mai scoffed. "Where can we go?"

"No choice but my house," Ray said, leading her away.

His rusty sedan sputtered to a stop under the noisy interstate overpass. A train thundered by on the railroad tracks behind them. Ray nodded to a shack in front of the headlights.

"Home sweet home," he said. Then added with mocked pride, "It's time you meet the family."

Mai caught her foot on a loose board on the porch step, but Ray steadied her. Only one hinge held the torn screen door in place. Ray pretended to tiptoe in, with Mai's hand in his. A heavy-set Hispanic woman lay in the dark, on the couch, watching a blaring TV. She sat up slowly. "Who's there?"

"It's just me, Ma. Ray."

She snapped on the shade-less lamp beside her. "Who you got there?"

"This is MaiLy."

"Oh," his mother stood, straightening her duster. "How nice to meet you," she sang. She staggered to greet Mai. Her breath smelled like liquor. "Can I get you a drink?"

"No thanks, Ma." Ray shook his head and looked apologetically at Mai.

"It's nice to meet you, Mrs. Martinez." Mai extended her hand.

His mom waved it away. "Lucy, call me Lucy. Here sit, sit."

She straightened the worn throw cover on a sagging, over-stuffed chair and motioned for Mai to be seated. The shag carpet was worn flat in front of the furniture. Dust covered every surface.

Mrs. Martinez swayed slightly, then said abruptly, "If you'll excuse me, I was just getting ready for bed."

She left the room and returned with two worn blankets. "You kids can sleep here on the floor. Good-night."

"Don't mind Ma," Ray said meekly. "She's under the weather. She gets under the weather just about every night." He spread the frayed blankets on the floor. "Guess we might as well hit the hay, too." Then he plopped down on the blanket and used couch cushions for pillows. "This'll have to do."

Reluctantly, Mai walked to the blanket and lay down with her back to him. She stiffened slightly when she felt him touch her hair.

"Good-night," Ray said.

"Good-night."

The whirring of traffic overhead and rumbling of passing trains eventually lulled Mai to sleep.

A blasting whistle woke her at dawn. She was used to waking up in strange places by now, but not accustomed to staring into strange little faces when she did.

"Hi, I'm Rosie. I'm four. Who are you?" Her dark brown eyes danced with merriment inappropriate for this hour of the morning. It looked as if she'd slept in the same dirty clothes she'd worn the day before.

Mai sat up slowly, brushing the hair from her face. "I'm MaiLy. A friend of Ray's," she whispered.

"What you doing on the floor?" Rosie chimed out loud.

"Just sleeping." Mai couldn't help but smile.

"You're pretty."

"Thank you." Mai ran her fingers through her hair again.

"Here comes Nicole. She's ten." She pointed to her sister walking down the hall, sucking her thumb, and wearing a Cabbage Patch Kids nightgown, too small for her. Nicole curled up on the corner of the sofa.

Rosie turned back to Mai. "Will you fix us breakfast?"

Since MaiLy had no idea what to do next, she welcomed the suggestion.

"Sure." She got to her feet while Ray slept, apparently undisturbed. "What do you have for breakfast?"

"Usually just cereal," Rosie said cheerfully. "Come on, Nicole."

Nicole followed them through the open doorway and sat silently on the chrome chair, her thumb still in her mouth.

Rosie pulled out several cabinet drawers and used them as steps to stand on the counter top. Reaching above the stove, she pulled down a box of Cocoa Krispies. Mai opened a carton of milk from the refrigerator, but the sour smell made her close it immediately. Rosie snickered at Mai's wrinkled nose.

"That's okay. We can just eat it dry again," Rosie reached into the box and shoved a fist full of cereal into her mouth.

Ray was leaning against the door jam, smiling. "I see you met the rest of the family."

"Nope, she didn't meet Daddy yet," Rosie offered. "He's still sleepin'."

"And probably will be 'til noon," Ray said. "Let's go, Mai. I got appointments to keep today."

"Sure," Mai headed for the living room and her purse. "What kind of appointments?"

"Business," he said. "Kind of private." Then he whispered. "A way to get me out of this hell hole."

Mai said good-bye to the girls and left with Rosie still perched on the counter top munching cereal and Nicole sitting in the chair, speechless and motionless, with her thumb in her mouth.

Ray dropped Mai at Shelly's. When Mai saw both Cadillacs gone from the driveway, she sneaked in the back door and into Shelly's room. She used Shelly's bathroom to shower, knowing nothing would wake her friend for hours. Then she flopped onto the extra bed in Shelly's room and slept until mid-afternoon. At four o'clock, she called Marcie at home, explaining that she hadn't been able to meet her lately and likely wouldn't for a while. Then she left to meet Ray for another party.

There he introduced her to another group of friends -- and to marijuana. She was the only person there who was not Hispanic. Ray convinced her that if she were to share a joint with them, they would all accept her like family.

"I could use some family!" Mai laughed nervously, then inhaled deeply.

She spent several days and nights there, feeling higher and happier than she had in years. Someone suggested that if she liked pot, she'd love cocaine. And she did, even when she woke in vomit.

At the end of the week, Ray insisted they go back to his parents' house again.

Mai was perplexed and embarrassed by their greeting.

"Get out of here!" Ray's mom yelled from the couch. Her speech was garbled. "You think you can just come and go as you please? Well, you're wrong!" She swayed to her feet and waved her arms toward the door. "Now get out and take your slut with you!"

Ray wrapped his arm around Mai's waist and guided her out the door, avoiding the pillow his mom hurled at them.

"Don't pay any attention to her. We'll just sleep in the car tonight. That's what I always do when she gets this way." He opened the back car door and motioned for Mai to get in. "She won't even remember this tomorrow when she sobers up. She'll be sweet as pie." He crawled into the front seat and lay down. "Good night."

The rumbling of traffic and trains could not lull Mai to sleep this time as she lay awake wondering, *Where am I, and where on God's earth am I going?*

CHAPTER 29

Ray was right. The next day Lucy was as sweet as pie. She welcomed Mai for supper and talked like they were old friends. Joe, Ray's dad, only grunted occasional responses to his wife's chattering.

Lucy yammered on about her janitorial job where she worked evenings and nights for good pay and benefits. It's a good thing, too, she declared, since Joe had been between jobs for over a year now and she couldn't count on her son for any help. He was a bum and always would be, she said in front of Ray.

Joe went "out" immediately after supper and Ray left for an "appointment." Nicole and Rosie were asleep on the couch as Lucy left for work.

"Can you keep an eye on the girls for me tonight, MaiLy?" Lucy purred.

And so the routine began. Most evenings Lucy went to work, Joe and Ray went "out," and Mai babysat the girls. Mai didn't mind missing the parties and nightly drug fests. She was almost disappointed to realize her alcohol consumption would continue -- with Ray's parents, now, instead of her friends. Beer washed down every supper, and whiskey followed into the evenings.

Mai and Ray continued to sleep together on the living room floor. Mai wondered whether the fact that they had never made love was due to the lack of privacy or the lack of love. She felt slightly rejected, yet greatly relieved.

Three weeks into this new living arrangement, she and Ray fell into their usual stuperous sleep.

"Police!" the cop bellowed as the front door crashed open in pieces.

Mai sat up and screamed. Before Ray could move, two officers drug him to his feet.

"Ray Martinez, we have a warrant for your arrest. You have the right to remain silent."

"I'm sorry, MaiLy," Ray interrupted. His sad brown eyes glared with fear and remorse as his arms were jerked behind his back and handcuffed. He looked at Mai huddled on the couch, wrapped in a blanket. Two policemen shoved him toward the door.

"Anything you say can and will be used against you in a court of law…"

Mai threw sweat pants and a sweatshirt on over her pajamas and followed them to the porch. She was about to cry out when she heard Nicole and Rosie whimpering behind her.

She tried not to scream, "Ray what's happening? Officer, what are the charges?"

"Parole violation and petty theft."

Mai couldn't comprehend what she was hearing. Before she could ask the million questions whirling in her head, Lucy and Joe came to the door.

"He ain't never amounted to nothin'." Lucy spit out the words. "Go ahead and take him. And keep him this time."

Mai approached the squad car as the officer placed his hand on Ray's head and eased him into the back seat. Lucy scoffed and walked back inside, with Joe following behind her.

As the police car pulled away, Ray looked at Mai one last time, his eyes pleading for compassion and forgiveness.

Two months later, Mai was able to visit Ray for the first time at the State Penitentiary in Canon City. She hoped his dilapidated Chevy would make the three-hour trip. Lucy and Joe had refused to come along, saying prisons made them nervous. Courtrooms made them nervous, too, so Mai had sat alone with Ray when the sentence was read --two years, without parole

She had gotten just one letter from Ray since they led him out of the courtroom in handcuffs. In his childlike handwriting, he said he was sorry for not telling her about the three years he'd served for burglary. He said he had planned to steal from only a few houses, and sell enough goods to get his own place. But the cops caught him on his second robbery. Possession of a controlled substance had been the second charge. That she understood too well.

The old Chevy chugged up Monument Pass and Mai smiled at the aspen trees shimmering like gold against the mountain pine. But the beauty and serenity of autumn did little to ease the ache in her heart. Her birthday was last week and no one knew or cared. At home there would have been ice cream and cake served on a musical platter. The whole family would have sung along, then applauded as a stack of presents was presented to her. Most gifts weren't store bought, but hand-made crafts or favorite personal items shared. Instead, Mai had spent her birthday working a ten-hour shift at the grocery store.

Lucy and Joe had suggested she could stay with them until Ray got out of prison, if she'd help pay expenses. She worked the day shift in the produce department so she could be home in time to babysat Rosie and Nicole in the evenings. At first, her days off were spent scrubbing and cleaning the house. Part of her first paycheck bought cleaning supplies and a used vacuum cleaner. The rest of it was spent on flowered bed sheets to cover the furniture, and for rugs to hide the bare spots on the carpet. Lucy seemed indifferent to the improvements, but Rosie and Nicole were excited with the new look and even took turns vacuuming the shabby carpet.

Mai rolled her window down to breathe in the crisp autumn air. The smell of the pine trees took her back to Dalat. An illusive peacefulness flirted with her heart, but vanished when she saw the State Prison exit looming ahead. She followed the signs and found the ominous fortress lurking on the far edge of Canon City.

With trembling hands she locked the car, then followed posted directions through the security check. The guard there rummaged through the contents of her purse dumped on top of the table. Then she was ushered to a visitor's area and took a chair in front of a glass window. She had braced herself for this meeting, but was still shocked to see Ray approach the other side of the glass wearing a prison uniform. The smile on his lips was not reflected in his eyes. His hair hung past his shoulders and he had a small goatee and mustache.

They engaged in awkward small talk for a while. He asked about his sisters, then about his mom and dad. When he learned Mai was working to pay the rent, he gritted his teeth.

"Don't let them use you, Mai. You shouldn't have to baby sit and pay rent, too."

"I'm lucky they'll let me stay with them. It's the least I can do."

"You should go home to your own parents, Mai. You deserve a better life."

"No, I don't," Mai heard herself say. "Besides, I can't let your family down now."

Ray shook his head slowly. "You're too good to them." He smiled again. "And too good to me, too. I never had nobody care for me the way you do. I still don't get it."

Mai shrugged. "Until I ran away, I'd never had a time in my life that no one cared for me. Even in the orphanage, the nuns cared for me. Then Pete found me and cared for me. Now it's my turn to care for somebody else. That's why I bought Rosie and Nicole clothes for school."

Ray interrupted. "You did?"

"Sure. Your folks couldn't afford it. I remember what it's like to be a little girl and have no pretty clothes of my own. I can still remember the day Dad and Mom came to the orphanage to take me out for the day. They brought me a beautiful, ruffled dress. I felt like a princess." Mai's mind and voice wandered as she enjoyed a glimpse of one of her favorite daydreams. "It makes me feel good to give your sisters that same feeling."

"I love you, MaiLy." Ray said, as if it had taken all his courage to speak. "Will you wait for me two years?"

"What else can I do?" Mai said lamely.

CHAPTER 30

The years passed quickly, probably because Mai was so busy with her second part-time job at the discount store. When Lucy announced she'd been laid off at work, it was obvious Mai's grocery store income could not pay all the expenses. Since Lucy could watch her own kids now, she suggested Mai should take on another job to help make ends meet. As long as the money kept coming in, Lucy was kind to MaiLy. But if funds were less than expected, she was belligerent. To keep peace, and to avoid conflict in front of the girls, Mai handed over nearly every cent she made.

Joe had hinted frequently, that he'd always wanted a stereo system. He seldom spoke, let alone asked for anything. So Mai surprised him with a five-piece component set. The monthly payments were small, and Mai told herself, it was the least she could do to help pay her own way.

Mai grew fond of Rosie and Nicole, even though their affection for her seemed directly related to the amount she spent on them. She lost fifteen pounds coping with her new life style, and Nicole, who was nearly eleven, loved

166

borrowing her clothes. That expectation fed closeness that had never existed between them.

Mai felt guilty for the small amount of money she stashed away and sent Ray to spend in the commissary, and even worse for the cash she hid to use when she went out.

Occasional drug binges with Ray's friends gave her the refuge she was seeking. Nightly drinking rituals with Ray's parents made life with them tolerable.

Mai knew better than to let her family know where she was living, but she did tell Marcie about her job at King Soopers Grocery. She was delighted when her siblings' occasionally took the bus clear across town to visit her in the produce department. Erica rarely came but David and Sara always greeted Mai with hugs and begged her to come home. Marcie had given up asking. Instead she filled her sister in on the family news.

One day Marcie exclaimed, "We're adopting two more kids!"

"What?" Mai froze, a bag of carrots in each hand.

"They're eight and nine. But not brother and sister like David and Sara. They're from India."

Mai was bewildered by her sister's obvious excitement. "Why are they adopting more kids? You'd think they would've learned their lesson after adopting me."

"You know Mom and Dad, MaiLy. They love kids, especially those who need a home. And despite what you may think, we have a great one to offer." Marcie grinned and hugged her sister. "Besides, you seem to be the only one who thinks adopting you was a bad idea."

With that, Marcie was off, leaving MaiLy slamming carrots onto the display and wondering why she was feeling so angry and confused. She had to admit she missed her home and frequently daydreamed about going back. She was tired of sharing a bed with Rosie or Nicole, but knew they needed her. And so did Lucy and Joe. And so did Ray. And when he got out of prison, she'd have a better home for

him to come to. She knew what is was like to be abandoned
- - she could never do that to him.

Ray wrote once a month for the entire two years, and
Mai always wrote back. She blamed her failure to visit him
regularly on her working two jobs and keeping a home.

One week before her twentieth birthday, Ray was
released from prison.

CHAPTER 31

Ray walked out of the prison gates wearing the same grubby shirt and pants he'd worn in. *Nothing has changed,* Mai thought as she watched him wave and saunter to the car where she was standing. She didn't know what she expected to feel when he hugged her, but when he did, hollow disappointment engulfed her. She loosened her embrace and started to speak, but his lips pressing forcefully on hers stopped her words. His hands moved down her back to her hips, pressing her to him.

"It's so good to see you," he breathed. "I ain't never had nobody wait for me before."

"I told you I'd be here," Mai said gently pushing him away. She reached for the car door. "Let's go home."

He jerked her back into his arms and kissed her too hard, then jogged to the passenger side of the car. "You better drive," he grinned. "I can't afford no tickets now."

Mai turned the key and pumped the pedal several times before the sputtering Chevy started.

"It's going to be different now, MaiLy," Ray was saying. "I'm turning over a new leaf. No more jail for me."

169

"Good, Ray," Mai said as she maneuvered the jalopy out of the prison complex. "Things are different at home now, too. I've got the place fixed up some and your folks are much nicer now."

"That's only because you're paying all the bills, Mai. I been thinking. We need to get our own place."

"No, you need to stay and work things out with your parents, Ray. They love you in their own way. They just don't know how to show it."

"That's for sure." Ray stared out the window. "I can get us some big money, then we'll move out on our own."

"You've got to stay out of trouble, Ray..."

"Oh, I will," he interrupted. "I learned a lot in prison. I know how to stay out of trouble, now. And I'll report to my parole officer every week."

For the remainder of the drive to Denver, Ray fantasized out loud about their great future together.

"Welcome home!" Lucy hollered as they entered the house. She raised her beer can in a salute, and Joe did the same. Mai wished they would greet him with a hug, but realized she had never seen any if them touch that way. Rosie and Nicole stood across the room holding up the small welcome home signs Mai helped them make.

"We bought a special supper to celebrate," Lucy said as she set a cardboard bucket of chicken on the table.

"Thanks, Ma." Ray said sincerely, then smiled. "I know this is your specialty."

"Well, it ain't everyday your son gets out of prison." Then she glared at Ray. "How many more prison-release parties you aimin' to have."

Ray hung his head. "None, Ma."

"Good!" Lucy cheered. "Then I propose a toast. To my son, the ex-con - - Raymond Rudolph Martinez."

"Rudolph?" Mai blurted as everyone raised their glasses.

"That's my Dad's middle name and his dad's too."

"See to it you do the name proud, this time," Joe spoke.

"That'll be the day," Lucy muttered

The evening was spent watching a rented video on the new VCR Mai had bought. She seemed to be the only one who felt the explicit sex in the movie was inappropriate for Rosie and Nicole. Ray enjoyed the feature too much. Mai held his hands to keep him from pawing at her body as they sat together on the couch. Whiskey and cigarettes were shared and even Nicole was allowed to join in now that she was thirteen.

At the end of the movie, Lucy staggered off to bed with Rosie trailing behind. Ray and his dad pulled Nicole to her feet and dragged her to her room. Ray returned with worn blankets and pillows and made their usual makeshift bed on the floor. He pulled the string on the floor lamp so the room was lit only by the streetlight filtering through the bent Venetian blinds. He took of his shirt and jeans and lay on the floor with his arms outstretched. Mai reached for the whiskey bottle, swigged three gulps, then walked to the blanket and lay beside him in her clothes. The first kiss was gentle. Then his hands and mouth groped her body roughly.

As she whimpered beneath him she knew Connie had been right. There is a difference between making love and having sex.

The blaring train whistle provided the customary wake-up call. Mai scurried to the bathtub where she soaked longer than usual. She dressed quickly and quietly, hoping Ray wouldn't wake before she left. From the porch she noticed an early autumn snowfall blanketing every building, twig, and blade of grass. She wished somehow her inner soul could capture the purity and peacefulness the scene offered.

Fortunately, the Chevy started on the third try. As she drove to work she convinced herself that Ray's love for her was all she needed. "After all," she scolded, her breath puffing white clouds, "in Vietnam I learned not to expect much love. Why should I expect more now." At the stoplight she rested her head on the steering wheel. "Besides, I'm probably getting all the love I deserve."

When the light changed, the car jerked forward. "I'll make the best of it. This is Ray's new start and I can make it work for him."

At work she bought makings for a spaghetti dinner then stopped for a bottle of wine on the way home. She used a sheet for a tablecloth then set it with the mismatched plates, flatware and Burger King glasses. Even Lucy was impressed with the preparations. Rosie helped tear lettuce for the salad.

Mai heard Ray come in the door and stomp snow from his shoes. She turned from the stove to see him standing with a bouquet of flowers in his hands. Without a word, he walked to her and kissed her lightly. "I might not be so good at showing it, but I do love you, MaiLy."

Mai threw her arms around his neck and stood in silence. He loved her alone. She had shared the nuns' love at the orphanage and her parents' love at home. This love was undivided.

She placed the flowers in an empty mayonnaise jar for a centerpiece. As she called the family to dinner she chided to herself, *See, MaiLy, everything's going to be just fine.*

But things weren't fine.

Four weeks later the police arrested Ray for parole violation. He had failed to keep his last two appointments with his parole officer and eventually confessed to stealing a case of beer. He had no answer to Mai's repeated pleas for an explanation.

Still, she paid his bond.

She sat next to him in the courtroom.

She trembled when the gavel pounded his six-month sentence.

She nodded "yes" when he was led from the courtroom begging, "Will you wait for me MaiLy?"

"You might as well stay on," Lucy said, "as long as you pay your way."

Where else would I go, Mai wondered. *I can't go back to Mom and Dad's - - not with my life in such a mess.* Having Ray's poor family seemed better than no family at all.

When the Chevy chugged its last polluting breath, Mai knew she had no choice. She had to rely on Lucy or Joe to take her to work so she could make enough money to accept their hospitality.

An ice storm glazed the streets when they picked her up after work one early December evening. The back seat was loaded with junk, so Lucy scooted next to Joe, allowing little room for Mai to wedge in and slam the door. The car reeked like a brewery, which explained Joe's impatience in the rush hour traffic. Cars and trucks skated warily through the sleeting snow.

Obviously exasperated with the icy congestion and Lucy's incessant directions, Joe made a sharp turn and sped recklessly down a side street. The traffic light ahead turned red. He jammed the brakes sending the car spinning in circles down the middle of the street. Mai covered her face and screamed as scenery spun at tilt-a-whirl speed. Then her side door flew open, hurling her flailing body over parked cars and onto the concrete sidewalk. At the same instant, a pickup collided into the side of the car where she'd been sitting, crashing both vehicles to a halt.

"Call the cops!" the cursing truck driver yelled to a gawking pedestrian as he rammed his way out of his concaved door.

"Call an ambulance!" a woman screamed as she bent over Mai's twisted, stone-still body, smashed against the snow-covered cement steps of a church. Blood seeped from her nose. Bone protruded through the flesh of her contorted right leg. A vessel in her neck pulsed the only hope of life.

Light glimmered from the stained glass window of Our Lady of Fatima Church. "Call the priest!" the woman yelled, then took off her coat and covered Mai, protecting her lifeless body from the storm.

The sounds of distant sirens coaxed Mai to a semi-conscious state. Images of Vietnam and running from the war shot through her mind. Instinctively, she tried to move her leg and her cries became audible. Her opened eyes begged for answers as she trembled in freezing fear. She felt the sleeting snow pellet her face and welcomed the numbness that deadened the rest of her body.

Ambulance personnel raced to her, shouting instructions and cutting her clothes off. She felt an oxygen mask over her face, and an IV jabbed into her arm. When her fractured leg was moved, she began to drift into a merciful state of unconsciousness; one she assumed to be death. Before succumbing she begged, "Forgive me God. Please save me."

"You're going to be okay," she heard a distant voice say. She woke to see an ambulance attendant smiling down at her. Pain broke through the numbness and Mai cried out as they turned her to her side and onto a backboard. That's when she saw the image of the Virgin Mary glowing colorfully in the church window.

The paramedic brushed a tear from Mai's cheek. "You're going to be okay," he repeated softly.

Mai stared at the stained glass Mary. "Yes, I am," she whispered.

"You really should take your pain pills," the heavyset nurse coaxed as she adjusted the traction suspending Mai's casted right leg.

Mai winced. "Not right now."

"Honey, anyone recovering from fractured ribs, a broken leg, and a concussion needs pain pills. Now, here." With a wink, she poured the medicine into Mai's palm.

"They make me sleepy, and I want to be awake in case somebody comes."

"Mai," the nurse almost whispered. "No one has come to see you in the two weeks you've been here. Visiting hours are over, but I promise, if someone comes, I'll wake you."

"Okay," Mai sighed. "I was just hoping, since today's Christmas ..."

The nurse handed Mai her water glass. "Isn't there someone you want me to call? You once mentioned your mom and dad and several brothers and sisters. Are you sure they know you're here?"

Mai avoided the question and the painful answer. She'd left them. They didn't know.

"Please take your pills so you don't hurt so much," the nurse insisted.

Mai swallowed the tablets, and turned her head to the wall. The nurse left leaving the door open a few inches so the sound of carolers drifted in from the hallway.

"So you don't hurt so much." Mai chuckled to choke back tears. "I wish there were a pill I could take for the real pain." Since she knew Lucy and Joe had walked away from the accident, Mai couldn't understand why they hadn't come to see her even once. Hospitals probably make them nervous too, she decided. Lucy had called the first day Mai was out of intensive care. She said Joe was using a cane and she was in terrible pain from her neck brace, so they wouldn't be able to visit for a while.

The Christmas carolers neared Mai's door. Their music took her back to the gates of Domani de Marie. She longed for the voices of the nuns' choir, for the tap on the head by Sister Katrine, for the pine cone decorations on the orphanage tree, for the kazoo harmonizing with her daddy as he performed his annual recital of Rudolph the Red Nosed Reindeer, for the clay gifts David and Sara had made her, for Connie's traditional reading of *The Night Before Christmas*.

Mai buried her head in her pillow and sobbed herself to sleep.

CHAPTER 32

"Happy New Year!" Mai and her favorite nurse chorused as they tapped their Styrofoam cups together.

"Is that a promise?" Mai droned.

"From all you've told me, this year has got to be better than last. Another week of physical therapy and you'll be home, running races on those crutches." The nurse finished her ginger ale. "That's all for me. I'm on duty," she said with her usual wink, then left the room humming Auld Lang Syne.

Mai snapped off the light and lay in the empty darkness, hugging herself. "This year has got to be better than last."

When she picked Mai up from the hospital, Lucy was wearing a neck brace and complaining about the pain she lived with daily. Joe couldn't work since he still used a cane and she worried out loud about how they could make ends meet now.

So Mai convinced her manager at King Soopers she could perform her job in a walking cast, and returned to work the next week.

As hard as it was going back to work, it was easier than staying home with Ray's family.

Ray was angry when Mai finally phoned and told him about the accident, and furious that his parents had kept it from him for months. He promised to get a good job when he was released so they could get a place of their own.

Springtime germinated hope for Mai. Her heart, like the flower buds, enfolded a promise of reformation. Her cast was off, her therapy complete, her strength renewed.

She had earned enough money to pay the bills, buy a used car, and start a secret savings account for her and Ray's fresh start together. When he was released he spent every day from morning to night looking for work. Lucy and Joe seemed happier without the burden of financial worries, so the whole family interacted more kindly than ever before.

Ray said his love for Mai grew in prison, and, it seemed, so did his need to express it. But daytime hugging and gentle kissing quickly dwindled, leaving only nighttime lovemaking as proof. It seemed to Mai that the act of sex, for Ray, was just that. As much as she hated his nightly drinking, she was grateful for the stupor that put him to sleep early. Most nights, she fought her drowsiness and pretended to be interested in late night television, to avoid going to bed with him. She convinced herself that their lives and their loving would improve when they got their own home and lives together.

But all the budding hope that sprouted in May withered in June.

Mai came home from work to find patrol car lights flashing the end of any promise. She dropped her bags on the sidewalk and stood dumbfounded as Ray was led out of the house, his hands cuffed behind his back.

"No, no, no." Her whispers gained volume. "No!"

"Sorry, MaiLy," Ray muttered, his eyes cast downward. "They got me for reckless driving is all, then found some drugs on me."

Immobilized by the anger and pity battling inside her, MaiLy watched as the officers nudged Ray into the back seat of the police car.

As it sped away, the anger won.

She took a deep breath and screamed until it was gone, "No!"

Mai was unable to resist Ray's pleas to be with him at the sentencing. "I got nobody, MaiLy," he begged. "Only you. Don't leave me now."

But this time Mai had refused to pay his bail.

This time she couldn't promise to visit and write often.

This time she couldn't pledge to wait for him eight months.

She went back to stay with his family only until she could sort out her feelings and her life. Determined to make it on her own, she took a second job at the discount store, again. That money would be saved until she could afford her independence.

The long hours exhausted her until physical symptoms took their toll. No one in the family seemed concerned with her weight loss and overwhelming fatigue. Mai forced herself to go to work each long day, then fell into bed with Nicole or Rosie at night.

Her six o'clock alarm demanded another day of work and illness.

"MaiLy, hurry up!" Nicole banged on the bathroom door. "What's takin' you so long?"

Mai hung her head over the toilet, vomiting. She moaned and used the seat cover as a headrest. The spinning room churned her stomach and its contents emptied again.

Nicole pounded her fist on the door, then barged in. "What's wrong with you?" Then she turned toward the hall and hollered, "Ma! Mai's puking in the toilet!"

Lucy shuffled down the hall in her faded nightgown. Curlers poked from beneath her torn hair net. She snarled, "What's wrong with you, MaiLy? I'm sick of you being sick!"

Mai wiped her mouth with a bath towel and pushed her hair back from her clammy face. "I'll be okay. It always goes away in a little while."

Lucy's jaw stiffened. She glared. "You puke every morning?"

"Almost."

"Damn it, girl!" she yelled. "You pregnant?"

"No!" Mai slammed the seat of the toilet down. "I'm just sick! Leave me alone." Shoving past Lucy and Nicole, she stomped down the hall, and collapsed onto her bed. She had missed her period last month, but blamed it on the stress of the new job. That had happened before. She couldn't be pregnant. She couldn't be.

Now there was pounding on the bedroom door. "Go to a doctor, then!" Lucy bellowed. "I'm sick and tired of you being sick and tired!"

"Ray?" Mai rested her aching head on the cool glass of the phone booth.

"MaiLy?" His voice peaked with excitement.

"Ray, we've got to talk." Mai slumped onto the narrow bench and held her nauseous stomach. She wondered whether fear or feebleness was causing her heart to pound so.

"Oh, Baby, it's so good to hear your voice. I miss you so much," Ray crooned.

"Ray, we have to talk," Mai repeated firmly. Then, before she lost her nerve, she blurted, "I'm pregnant."

There was no response.

"Did you hear me? I'm pregnant!" she shouted to keep tears at bay. "I don't know what to do," she choked.

Ray's silence fueled her confusion and hopelessness, then her anger.

I never should have told him, she seethed. *I don't need this. And I don't need him. You don't have to be upset, Ray Martinez. I can do this without you.*

Before she could shout it, he spoke. "I'm so happy, MaiLy. This is the greatest news of my life!"

"Great news?" Mai yelled. "How can you say that? My whole world is falling apart, and you think it's great news!"

"It is great!" he cheered. "I'll be out before the baby's born and we'll take care of it together."

"Ray, we can't take care of ourselves. How can we take care of a baby?" She paused. "I thought about having an abortion."

Ray hollered so loud Mai held the phone away from her ear. "No way, MaiLy!"

"I don't know what to do," Mai sniffled. "Sometimes I put my hand on my belly and try to wish the baby away."

"Mai, I promise, when I get out this time, I'll be straight and clean. I'll take care of you and the baby."

"I want to believe you, Ray. But every time I do, it's a lie."

"I ain't lying this time, Mai. I swear." Then his voice softened. "My family know?"

Mai covered the phone with her hand until she could compose herself, then said, "Your mom called me a stupid whore."

"Damn her! She's the stupid one, MaiLy. I told you before, don't pay no attention to her."

"Nicole gave me ginger to eat and told me to drink black coffee to get rid of the baby."

"Damn her, too! How does she know all that, anyway?"

"Your little sister knows more than you think. Your dad's the one who helped me. He helped me see things straight."

"My dad?"

"Yes. He said he wasn't the smartest guy on earth, but did know taking one life can't make another one better. That's when I quit trying to hurt my baby and help it." That said, Mai cried uncontrollably. Finally she added, "I quit the drugs - - and drinking, too."

When she finally hung up the phone, she sat a long time in the quiet booth, wishing she could stay forever in this reclusive hideout, away from the chaotic, troubled world outside. As she soaked in the temporary peacefulness, Mai rubbed her lower abdomen gently. A faint smile curved her lips.

Lucy was livid when she learned Mai had spoken to Ray and decided against an abortion. "That boy is no good." She drilled her cigarette butt into the ashtray on the kitchen table. "You'd leave him now, if you know what's good for you." She lit another cigarette and squinted her eyes. "If you think you can stay here with a baby, you got another thing coming. We're barely getting by now. No way we can afford another mouth to feed."

"As soon as I can, I'm getting my own place." Mai shoved her chair away from the table. "Then you can feed all the mouths!"

Her coworkers didn't seem to notice her tummy bulging beneath her smock. Shame and worry made her hide the truth from herself and others. Yet there were moments she wanted to stand on top of a mountain, or at least a fruit display, and shout to tell the world about the life growing inside her. She spent hours resting her hands on her abdomen, feeling her baby nudge her along.

Marcie stopped by the store frequently, again, and Mai knew it was only a matter of time before she saw the obvious. When Mai had told her about the accident and her long hospitalization, Marcie seemed more hurt than angry.

"So that's where you were. I came several times and didn't see you here, so I figured you quit. We all just kept praying we'd hear from you over the holidays. When are you going to learn we care about you, MaiLy?" Marcie scolded. "Promise me you will never go through something like that again without letting us know."

MaiLy was careful not to promise.

When Mai was in her sixth month, Marcie showed up at the store and surprised her with a hug that was unusually long and close. When she stepped back, she smiled and stared at Mai's protruding smock. "When are you due?"

"February."

Marcie squealed and hugged her sister again. "I'm going to be an aunt!" Then she grilled Mai on how she was feeling, whether she was getting good medical care, and what her plans were for delivery. Mai assured her that her job provided good insurance and she was seeing a competent obstetrician regularly.

"Oh, please come home," Marcie pleaded.

"I can't," Mai said as she rearranged the already perfect pyramid of oranges. "The family seems happy now. The last thing they need is me coming back with all my troubles."

"We are happy, Mai, especially with the addition of Nathan and Elizabeth. But don't you see? Our family's not complete without you."

"I can't," Mai said without looking up.

Several weeks later, Mai was wrapping brown bananas for the discount tables when she heard a man's voice softly call her name. Looking up, she gazed into the eyes of her dad.

"Hi, Honey," he said nervously.

"Dad."

"I hope it okay that I came here. I just had to see you." He reached one arm out in a gesture that seemed to offer not only his hand, but also peace. Mai grasped it and felt a surge of his strength and love flow through her.

"Oh, Daddy." She pulled his arm around her and wrapped hers around his neck, ignoring the stares of shoppers. His tears trickled on her neck as she clung to him. Then almost giggling, he held her at arm's length.

"You're beautiful," he whispered, then touched her belly. "So beautiful."

Suddenly the shame vanished and, for the first time in many months, beautiful is how she felt.

Mai's supervisor passed and smiled politely. Taking his cue, Pete said quickly, "I can't stay. I just wanted to give you this." He reached into his briefcase and pulled out a photograph album. "Mom and I made you this."

She held it reverently. "You made this - - for me?"

He helped her open the cover. There, pasted on the first page, were pictures of her at Domani de Marie. She looked into his beaming face as he turned the page and tapped at a photo.

"Look, this is you and me on the paddle boat ride." He chuckled. "Remember that day? I loved you so much and tried so hard to make you happy, but couldn't seem to figure out how."

Their stares locked.

The supervisor passed by again and didn't smile this time.

"There are pictures of our whole family in here," Pete said closing the book. "We want you to come for dinner, Mai. Any night you say."

"I don't know, Dad…"

"Please?"

Mai clasped the album to her chest. "I'm off on Friday."

Pete's whole face lit. "Friday then." Walking backwards and waving he repeated, "See you Friday. And, MaiLy - - I love you."

CHAPTER 33

Mai sat outside the two-story home with the car engine still running. The windshield quickly fogged over in the cold January night. She wiped the glass with her coat sleeve to see golden light glow from every window in the house; like a beacon calling her home. A dozen times she had decided not to come, but something, maybe this beacon, lured her.

Lucy was obviously threatened when she heard about Pete's visit and dinner invitation and she had suddenly become very kind and accommodating. "You and my grand baby are always welcome here," she had said. "And I can baby sit when you go back to work."

Ray would be out of prison in a few weeks, and Mai knew that together they would fit in with his family better than hers.

"It's only dinner," she said to herself as she turned off the ignition. During stressful times like these, Mai found herself longing for a drink. Yet, not once had she broken that promise to her baby.

She walked up the cobblestone path, pulling her coat around her the best she could. It didn't cover her front anymore, but she couldn't waste her money on a new one. With a few more paychecks she'd have enough saved to make a deposit on a place for her and Ray.

She could feel her heart beating in her neck and her baby somersaulted inside her as if anticipating the excitement. It felt strange to ring the doorbell, yet she knew she had no right to walk in as if this were still her home. She had relinquished that five years ago. The thunder of footsteps preceded the door flying open.

Eight people stood with open arms.

"MaiLy!" Sara squealed, hugging her first. Then David wedged his way into Mai's arms. At the same time Marcie cuddled her. "I'm so glad you're home."

Everyone babbled in unison as the first greeters stepped back. Pete's hug twirled her in a circle and deposited her in front of Connie who stood with outstretched arms.

Mai's frozen heart melted in the embrace of her mother.

By then the whole group was sniveling and laughing all at the same time.

"This is Nathan," David piped up, patting the head of his brother. "He and Elizabeth just got here before Christmas." Both children smiled, their dark brown hair and eyes shining.

"Welcome home." Erica stepped forward. Mai hesitated, then Erica flashed two fingers in a V. "Peace," she said, wrapping her arms around her sister.

The sniveling turned to blubbering.

"Enough already!" Connie finally said. "Dinner's ready. Let's eat!"

They all traipsed to the kitchen. Mai found her usual place at the table, which now had all the leaves in it. The chatter subsided quickly when everyone was seated. Heads bowed as Pete led them in their usual grace. At the end he simply added, "And thanks for having our whole family together."

As if the gun had fired at the starting gate, the children began snapping napkins, passing platters, and reaching for bowls of food. When the cackling accelerated, Pete suggested in a loud voice that everyone take a turn telling something about themselves. He started by announcing that he had been made full partner in the legal firm and, when the receptionist answered the phone, his name was finally at the end of the list. Then he turned to his son as if making an introduction. "David?"

David took a deep breath and rattled, "Buckingham, Panosh, Duello, Fritz, Cook, Lickens, MASON and Associates." The entire troupe howled with laughter at the obviously rehearsed and much loved performance.

Connie talked briefly about the broad scope of FVNC, now in ten countries. Mai thought her mom looked a little worn and tired, but knew her commitment to children - - her own and the world's - - would drive her harder still. She wondered how many children's lives had been saved by her mother's selfless, unceasing efforts.

The kids took turns telling about activities in sports and school. Nathan and Elizabeth spoke limited English, so Sara told about them. Mai smiled to see printed cards taped around the room, identifying all the kitchen objects. They were the same cards Marcie had made for her; tattered now, from nearly ten years wear.

When it was her turn, Mai plastered a smile on her face and exaggerated her enthusiasm about her two jobs and bulging savings account. She decided it best not to talk about the baby.

After supper, Mai wasn't surprised to see the same regimented routine for cleaning the kitchen. Someone shouted; "Go!" and the mad flurry of clattering pans and sloshing sponges began. Dishes were tossed down a line of workers like an old time fire bucket brigade. Marcie washed and rinsed each piece, then handed it to Sara to dry, then pass to Erica to put it in the cupboard. David pitched the catsup and mustard to Nathan who tossed them in the open refrigerator door. Soon, Marcie pulled the plug from the sink and triumphantly called out, "Done!"

"Eight minutes!" David proclaimed. "That's our record!"

Shaking her head and shrugging in mock despair, Connie herded the clan into the living room. Stacked on the coffee table were a dozen packages in baby wrapping paper.

"It's called a shower!" Sara announced.

Mai eased into the over-stuffed chair, made into a makeshift throne. Speechless, she shook her head in disbelief as she sat surrounded by her exuberant, loving family. One by one she opened presents for her child; blankets, sleepers, booties, diapers, each with a hand-made card.

At the end of the evening, the entire family helped carry the gifts to her car. There, they each kissed her good-bye and invited her back soon. Pete and Connie hugged her together. "This will always be your home," they said.

Mai shut the car door and started the engine. Her parents waved from the sidewalk as she pulled away and headed to the shack she called home.

The baby was due in only four weeks but Mai kept her grueling two-job schedule. She knew both employers assumed she had quit the other job. As her savings account grew, so did her fatigue. The bouncing baby inside her kept her awake most nights, but Mai didn't mind. She treasured the moments and shared her innermost feelings with her little one. The maternal love she already felt amazed her.

"I've got a lot to learn about loving a child," she whispered one night as she lay caressing her belly. Her parents' ability to forgive still baffled her. How could they welcome her back so lovingly after all she'd done? They had even offered to move her back home and prepare a nursery there. Mai couldn't explain to them, or herself, why she had refused. But their weekly phone calls and occasional dinners together brought a peaceful happiness only family could offer.

Her parents personified the unconditional love they had often talked about. "That's how I must learn to love," she said to her baby. "Especially Ray."

Her folks asked her to notify them at the onset of labor, which secretly eased Mai's worry. She had declined childbirth classes, refusing to sit with happy couples. "Oh, I'm not married," she could hear her own introduction. "You see, the baby's father is in prison, again..." So instead she read the books her doctor had suggested. Though she felt completely overwhelmed and unprepared, she already knew there was no challenge in this life that she and this baby couldn't conquer together.

Ray's parole officer picked him up at the prison and took him for a job interview before bringing him home. He reminded him that, while working at a fast food restaurant was not a glorious job, he was lucky to find someone willing to hire a parolee.

Ray ran up the snowy porch steps two at a time. He burst through the front door, took Mai into his arms, and spun around the room. He kissed her hard as his hands rubbed her back and hips.

Then, as if startled, he said, "Oh! The baby!" and softly patted her belly. "Are you okay, little fella?"

Mai put her arms around him and hugged him close again. Then, grabbing her coat she said, "There's something I want to show you before your folks get back. Take a walk with me."

"What is it?" Ray asked like an eager schoolboy.

"A surprise." Mai took his hand and led him outside and down the sidewalk. They walked four blocks, stopping several times to hug, while Ray expounded on what a great parent he would be. Every sentence seemed to begin with, "I won't be like my dad, I will..."

They stopped in front of a run-down apartment house. Mai dangled a pair of keys from her finger. "Apartment number four. Our new home. Our new lives together."

"You're kidding!" Ray stammered. But Mai's glowing smile confirmed the truth. His hug lifted her off the ground. He kissed her neck, her face, her forehead, saying, "Thank you, thank you, thank you."

They jogged across the barren lawn to the staircase in the back. The worn wooden railing matched the rest of the building.

"It's not much, but it's all we can afford right now," Mai said, turning the key. "It'll take both our wages to keep it. It's furnished," Mai waved her hand around the living room. "But I added a few homey touches." New throw covers in a Southwest design covered a sagging sofa and chair. A bouquet of straw flowers in complimenting colors adorned a scratched-up coffee table.

"There's just a tiny kitchen and only one bedroom," she said as they walked down a short hallway. "I found this comforter and matching curtains at a garage sale."

"It's great." Ray sat on the edge of the bed shaking his head. "I can't believe it."

A wicker bassinet sat in the corner. The Winnie the Pooh mobile Marcie bought danced above it.

Mai sat beside Ray and held his hand. "This is everything I've worked for, Ray. You have to help us keep it. I'll have to be off work awhile after the baby."

"I start flippin' burgers tomorrow," Ray said with sincere pride. "If I do good I'll be promoted to fry manager in just a few months."

"Your folks are sure we're never going to make it, Ray. They're mad we moved out. Now they're looking for jobs, but it seems to me they spend more time looking for welfare and disability payments."

"That's their problem. Now it's just you and me, Mai."

He leaned her back on the bed and kissed her. Opening her jacket, he fumbled with the buttons on her blouse. "Can we? I mean is it okay?"

"Just this once, the doctor said." Mai tried to take the tension from her voice. "Then no more 'til a couple months after the baby." Ray was already unzipping his jeans.

It wasn't really a lie, Mai told herself. The doctor had said, "Whenever you're comfortable."

As Ray's jeans dropped to floor Mai wondered, would she ever be comfortable?

A few days later, Mai left work early and went home to take a warm bath. The book was right; that usually eased her false labor contractions. But, not this time. She went to bed early, but slept little as the cramping continued with greater intensity. By morning the contractions were five minutes apart.

"Better not go to work, today, Ray. I think this is it."

The look of panic on his face matched that skipping in her heart. For weeks she had wished for this moment. Now she wondered why.

She phoned the doctor who asked her several questions, then directed her to the hospital. From there she would call her folks.

"Grab my suitcase from the closet, will you Ray? I have it all packed. Just have to add a few last minute things."

Ray hurled the luggage on the bed and opened it up side down, its contents jumbling into the lid. Then, darting around the room like a jackrabbit, he opened and slammed drawers, cramming items into the suitcase.

Mai managed a laugh. "Ray. I haven't worn these blue jeans in a year!" She nudged him aside. "Let me do this."

Satisfied she had everything suggested in the book, Mai snapped the bag shut and said, "Let's go have our baby."

Ray dashed ahead of her down the steps, banging the suitcase on every rail. Then he raced back to guide Mai down the steps, as if she were blind. "Step. Step. Turn. Eeeasy."

Mai had to drive since Ray's license was still revoked. She curled herself over the steering wheel and counted to herself as she breathed through each contraction. *In: two, three, four. Out: two, three, four.*

"Oohh!" Mai groaned. "I hope I can make it. They're getting harder and closer together!"

Ray used the cuff of his shirtsleeve to wipe sweat from Mai's face, then his. In twenty minutes, they arrived at the emergency entrance and were escorted to the Labor and Delivery Department. Mai offered Ray the wheelchair, but he walked along side her instead.

The contractions were stronger and longer. In between them, Mai phoned her parents. They were both out, so she left messages with their secretaries. Ray also called Lucy and Joe and told them not to come, but he would call again when the baby was born. When they learned Mai's parents were on their way, they insisted on coming, too.

For the next eight hours, Mai panted and breathed through the waves of pain as Ray sat helplessly at her side. He mopped her forehead with a wet cloth and spooned ice chips into her mouth. Lucy, Joe, and the girls watched TV in the waiting room. Connie and Pete alternated their pacing between there and the foot of Mai's bed.

"Where's my mother?" Mai had asked before Connie arrived. "I need her close."

When it was time to deliver, Mai was exhausted. Then the nurse coached, "Push this baby out and into your arms." A tremendous power surged through Mai. She was overcome by an extraordinary physical, emotional, and spiritual strength.

The nurse whispered into her ear, "This is about to be the greatest moment of your life."

"Push!" Ray echoed the doctor's command.

Then from her loins she delivered a new life.

"It's a boy!" the doctor cheered, placing the child on Mai's abdomen. With trembling hands, she reached for him and pulled him to her heart, exploding with love.

The nurse was right.

Tears rolled off her face onto his chubby arms. Mai stroked his black hair as his dark brown eyes gazed up at her. "I can't believe it," she said over and over again.

Tears brimmed in Ray's eyes as he touched his baby with his fingertip.

Connie and Paul tiptoed back into the room. Mai beckoned them to her. "I have a son!" she cried out loud. They leaned over her bed together to hug her. Pete extended his arm to welcome Ray into the embrace. Their tears mixed as they cradled a new love.

Ray wiped his nose with his shirtsleeve. Mai kissed his cheek and spoke only to him. "I named our son Rudy - - after you."

Ray buried his head in the pillow next to Mai and sobbed.

The nurse swaddled the baby in a blanket and put a tiny knitted cap on his head. While the doctor completed the birthing repairs, Ray carried his son to meet his parents. Then everyone gathered around Mai's bed to revel in the joy only babies could bring.

Finally, at the end of the day, Mai lay alone in the dark, caressing her son. The sweat of her labor had been purifying water for her. In her arms she held all she needed in the world.

She kissed the forehead of her new life.

CHAPTER 34

The next morning, Mai sat in bed feeding Rudy. As he suckled from her breast, she knew only she could nurture him. This filled her with a pride that deepened her love as she snuggled him close.

She hadn't slept much all night. Her body could not succumb to its fatigue as the events of the previous day replayed in her mind. Love and life's promises flowed- - from her parents, Ray's parents, and most of all, from Ray. She knew the birth of their son had transformed him forever, too.

Her door opened with a bang. "Good mornin' lil' Mama!" Ray said too loudly. He stubbed his toe on the bedside stand and cursed, and bent over to kiss her. Mai turned her head from his whiskey breath, then faced him again. "You're drunk!"

"No. Me and the boys just celebrated most of the night. It ain't everyday a guy becomes a dad."

"Ray, you promised…"

He raised his voice. "I know!" but lowered it again. "I'll be good." He fondled her swollen breasts and slurred, "Real good."

Mai shoved his hand away just as the nurse entered the room. "Everything okay, MaiLy?"

"Yes." She said with a counterfeit smile. "Ray was just going home for a shower and some sleep."

"That sounds like a good idea," the nurse said stepping between the bed and Ray.

"Good idea," Ray backed toward the door. He pointed a finger at Mai and winked. "And don't you worry. Everything's going to be great. I promise."

And things were great for the next few weeks. Ray took the bus to work every day and returned to enjoy Mai's home cooking each evening. Together they tended Rudy and loved and laughed their way through baby baths, stinky diapers, and sleepless nights. Mai loved the role of homemaker.

She was making a home, at last.

But her savings account dwindled too quickly. Instead of waiting the recommended six weeks, she went back to work in just two. Ray switched to the evening shift so he could watch baby Rudy during the day.

Mai felt her heart break whenever she left for work. While her body was in the produce department, her spirit was back at the apartment with her baby. She called home frequently to hear Ray's reassurance that things were going fine.

Occasionally, she came home to find Lucy caring for Rudy while Ray was out with a new friend, Max, looking for a job with better pay. While Mai had never met him, Max seemed to be a good influence on Ray. Whenever Ray spoke of him, he talked about setting higher expectations in life. Ray had even pointed out the affluent home where Max lived with his parents while his financial goals were being established.

Mai allowed herself to hope Max's motivation would rub off on Ray- -until she trudged up the stairs late one afternoon in March and heard rock music blaring from their apartment. Ray sat hunched in the middle of the living room floor with three empty beer cans at his side. He didn't know Mai was home until her fist punched the off button on the stereo.

Rudy was screaming in the bedroom.

She swept him into her arms and stormed out of the apartment. When she returned several hours later, a remorseful Ray begged forgiveness and pledged reform - - again.

Mai begged, too. "If we're going to make this work - - make a home - - I can't do it without you. I need you, Ray."

"And I need you, MaiLy."

But Mai's turmoil was short-lived.

Ray called from the police station within a few days.

Petty theft.

No bail.

Of course she had to stand beside the father of her child as the judge hammered an eighteen-month sentence.

Lucy and Joe persuaded Mai to move back in with them since she couldn't afford the apartment on her own. That money, Lucy insisted, could be used to pay for Rudy's childcare. And since Lucy was still looking for work, she would be willing to baby-sit for the going rate.

A single bed and crib would fit in the girls' bedroom if Rosie and Nicole had bunk beds. Mai, of course, purchased them since this arrangement was to accommodate her.

Mai moped through the next year. She imagined herself on the raft with Sister Katrine, fearing waves of depression and confusion would wash her away. Her son was all that kept her tethered. Just touching him gave her strength.

She went to work at 5:00 a.m. so she'd be off at 2:00 - - before Lucy and Joe began drinking. Lucy seemed to take good care of Rudy during the day, but was eager to relinquish the job when Mai got home. This suited Mai fine, because she loved caring for her son. She spent countless hours cuddling, rocking, and playing with him. The wheels on the used stroller wore thin from daily excursions around the neighborhood and parks.

Rudy's cries in the night evoked memories of Domani de Marie, where she had knelt and pleaded for a family. As she rocked him alone in the dark, she knew she held the answer to that prayer.

She cheered when he got his first tooth, and applauded when he sat up alone. As her child grew, so did her determination to provide a better life for him.

Visits to her family grew less frequent. She was embarrassed by her decisions and life style, yet was determined to manage without them. When they came into the grocery store, she always acted too busy to visit, and sometimes even hid. Mai joined them for dinner occasionally, but the love they showered on her and Rudy only heightened her guilt. Gradually, she became too busy to accept their invitations.

Mai didn't tell Lucy when she got a promotion at work. As a cashier, she now had better wages and benefits. She reestablished a secret savings account that would one day buy her independence.

Just weeks before his first birthday, Rudy took his first steps, and toddled into MaiLy's arms.

And so did Ray.

He was released from the county jail early because of overcrowding there. Mai had visited him only once that year and refused his request to bring Rudy along. With all the unconditional love she could muster, Mai welcomed him home and into her single bed. He repeated his usual promises of reformation, but her cautious, broken heart couldn't believe him.

"I'll prove it this time," he promised.

He brought her flowers several times a week and told her often how much he loved and needed her. Mai noticed an attempted tenderness in their infrequent love making behind locked doors.

Surely if she pretended to love him, it would eventually become real again.

His minimum wage job at the car wash was temporary, he said, until Max found him something better - - so he could support his family like a man. Ray seemed proud to help pay the rent and Lucy's childcare fee, so Mai was able to sneak extra money into her still-secret account. She enjoyed her job as a cashier and was flattered by the extra responsibility.

She greeted each customer with an enthusiastic smile. Her supervisor praised her attitude and her attention to detail. Though working with large sums of money, her cash drawer always balanced and the grumpiest shoppers left smiling. Her personal interactions with regular customers drew them to her line exclusively.

"Thank you, Dearie," the old lady said as Mai handed her the receipt and summoned for carryout.

The next man in line used his paycheck to buy his cart full of groceries. Following established protocol, Mai cashed his check and counted out the remaining change in large bills. He seemed to stare through her as she handed him the last of his money. His mustache quivered and his deep blue eyes darted as he stuffed the cash into the pocket of his Denver Bronco jacket.

He returned the next week and seemed equally uneasy when she cashed his check for his purchase. She thought it was a coincidence when, an hour later, she noticed him walking behind her when she left the store and headed to her car.

When she returned to work the next morning, a man with a mustache and Bronco jacket sat in a parked car in the employees' end of the parking lot. *It's still dark out,* she told herself. *It's impossible to recognize anyone at this hour.*

Three days later, when she arrived home after work, she thought she saw him again at the end of the block. "Lots of people have mustaches," she muttered to herself.

He waited in her line a few days later, even though the adjacent checkout row was empty.

"You live around here?" he asked as she cashed his weekly paycheck. His eyes seemed to flicker as he glared into hers.

Fear trickled through her. "Have a nice day," was all she said, then turned to greet the next customer.

The creepy guy seemed to disappear and, after a few weeks, Mai felt relieved when he hadn't returned to the store.

It wasn't until she was pushing the stroller, four blocks from home, that she saw him again. The early morning spring breeze was cool, so she faced Rudy to raise the hood on his little sweatshirt.

That's when she caught a glimpse of him walking nearly a half block behind her.

Mai quickened her step and headed for home. She glanced back to see him walking faster, coming closer. Her jog soon became a race as she ran behind the rickety stroller. Rudy's giggles told her he didn't sense the danger.

But she did.

She barely stopped at the corner to allow an old man in an old car chug through the intersection. Mai flashed a look over her shoulder before bolting ahead.

"Hey, you!" the stalker shouted.

Mai tore across the street. "It's okay, son," she wheezed to Rudy, who was beginning to whimper. "I'll protect you."

Those words hurled her back to the night she was assaulted.

The same pain and fear shot through her like electricity, charging her on even faster.

She was surprised at her own strength when she picked up the stroller, Rudy and all, and heaved it up the steps and into the house.

"What's the matter with you?" Lucy scolded, looking up from the TV.

Panting, Mai unfastened Rudy from the stroller and hustled him to the bedroom. Ray heeded her command to follow them.

Lucy grumbled and returned to her game show.

"Ray, someone is chasing me and Rudy!" she gasped. He sat beside her and put his arm around her as she told him, for the first time, about the creepy man.

"Why didn't you tell me? I would've found the guy and knocked his block off! Nobody's going to hurt my woman and kid!"

Mai wished he could have responded with gentle concern, but knew it wasn't in him.

Anger was.

"I think we should call the police," Mai reasoned.

Ray jumped up and paced in front of the bed. "Police is the last thing we need! Leave it to me. I can handle this!" he boasted.

A loud knock rattled the front door. They looked at each other with shared alarm. Mai opened the bedroom door a few inches and heard a muffled introduction. "Agent Thompson, FBI."

"FBI?" Mai hissed, easing the door closed. "Ray, now what did you do? Rob a bank? It's the FBI!"

Fear turned his face gray. "Nothin'. I swear!"

"MaiLy!" Lucy shrilled

Mai murmured as she walked out of the room, "What kind of a mess am I going to have to get you out of this time, Ray?"

A man in a business suit stood just inside the front door. "MaiLy Mason?"

"Yes."

LeAnn Thieman

"Agent Thompson, FBI. We have a warrant for your arrest."

"What?"

"Fraud by check, forgery, and money laundering."

"What?" Mai stumbled back onto Ray's shoulder. "There must be some mistake."

"No mistake." Then through the screen door he called, "Harold?"

The creepy guy in the Bronco jacket entered.

Mai slumped into Ray's arms and he almost dropped her as he lunged toward the man. "You son-of-a-..."

Two police officers ran in from the porch and grabbed Ray. "Easy, buddy."

Agent Thompson pointed to the creepy man. "This is Agent Harold Young. He's been undercover, tracking your activities for the past several months. I'm afraid you'll have to come with us. You have the right to remain silent..."

"There must be some mistake," Mai repeated, her trembling hands wiping her tears. "Ray, help me."

"Don't worry, Honey," Ray said as the officers drew Mai's wrists behind her back, and locked them. "No matter what you done, I'll stick by you, just like you stuck by me."

"Take care of Rudy!" she called as the officer placed his hand on her head and eased her into the patrol car.

200

CHAPTER 35

It only took one phone call.

"Daddy. Will you help me?"

Pete was at the station thirty minutes after Mai was fingerprinted and photographed. He found her in an interrogation room, her petite, beautiful body cowering in a chair next to a table as tall men in business suits loomed over her. Squatting beside his daughter, Pete hugged her a long time. Then he introduced himself to the men as Mai's father and attorney. "What's going on here?"

Agent Thompson explained that Mai was allegedly a key player in a fraudulent check-cashing scheme. Agent Young reported he had witnessed Mai using her position at the grocery store to cash checks for her accomplices. Pete listened as he recited the case, then simply said, "May I speak to my daughter alone?"

"Five minutes." Agent Thompson gestured his staff to follow him out of the room.

Pete sat next to Mai at the table. He caressed her hand in his and touched a tear from her cheek. He spoke in a hushed, gentle voice. "I will ask this only once, MaiLy. Are you involved in this in any way?"

"How can you even ask me that?" she snapped. "Do you believe them?"

Pete kept his voice low and even. "I believe you. That's why you must tell me the truth."

"No, Daddy, I'm not involved. I swear to God."

"That's all I need to know." He squeezed her hand. "One of my partners is on his way. We'll get you out of this. All you have to do is keep telling the truth, even when it's hard."

When the FBI agents reentered, Pete's partner, Tom Buckingham, was with them. Mai had known Tom since she was a little girl. His hug told her she was in good hands.

For the next three hours Mai answered questions fired at her and listened as the preposterous story unfolded. The store manager had accused her of being involved with the operation and cited her outstanding rapport with the customers as a device for deceit. What was her cut? He had wanted to know.

"Do you know Maxwell Murphy?" Agent Creepy Guy asked.

"No."

"Are you sure?" He slid a photograph across the table.

Mai shook her head. "I've never seen him before."

"Are you absolutely certain?"

Pete interjected, "If she said she doesn't know him, she doesn't.

"Well, he knows her. Our evidence suggests she worked for him."

"I don't know anyone named Max..." She stopped. "Wait. Ray has a new friend named Max!"

She told them everything she had ever heard about him, and the interview took a new direction. After two more hours of interrogation, she was instructed to write with her left hand, then her right.

The examination ended.

Adrift in the Storms

Pete posted bail, and they left.

Connie met them in the lobby. She wrapped her arms around MaiLy and kissed her cheek. "Let's go to your place and get Rudy and your things. You're coming home with us."

Mai paused only a second. Was Ray involved in this crime ring? Had he, like her boss, betrayed her loyalty? What was best for Rudy and her now? "Thanks, Mom," she sighed.

When Mai walked into the house with the empty boxes Connie had brought, Lucy began her usual rant. Then she saw Mai's parents on the porch and tromped to her bedroom and slammed the door.

Ray approached Mai with open arms. She pushed past him and headed to their bedroom where Rudy was napping in his crib.

"I was going to come down to the station with you, really I was, but with my parole and all..." Ray sputtered.

Without a word, Mai emptied dresser drawers into boxes. Ray grabbed her arm. "You ain't leavin' now, are you?"

"Yes, she is," Pete barked from the bedroom doorway. "Now take your hands off her."

Connie gathered up sleepy Rudy. Pete threw all the baby clothes in a box and said, "I'll be back for the rest of Mai's things; the crib, highchair, and everything else she bought. Now get out of our way."

He led his family through the door and to the car. They shoved boxes into the back seat and trunk. Connie put more cartons in Mai's car, then placed Rudy in his car seat and drove away. As Mai slid into her Dad's car, Ray stood on the curb looking like a spanked puppy.

"I love you, MaiLy," he whined. "I'll be waiting for you."

Pete glared at him with fiery eyes. "Don't."

Once again, her dad seemed to read her unspoken need and they rode in silence most of the way home. The crimson

203

sunset blushed the house with a warm, welcoming glow. Daffodils and tulips decorated the cobblestone walk as Pete held her hand, leading her home.

Inside she found Rudy already in Marcie's arms with the other children gathered around him. They greeted Mai as if nothing happened and her being there was a delightful, everyday occurrence. Stilted conversation at the dinner table made it obvious, though, they had all been coached on forbidden topics. With the day's events tumbling over and over in her mind, Mai sat glumly, poking at her food with her fork.

After supper, everyone helped carry boxes from the car to the basement. Mai was surprised to see a crib in the guest room there.

"Oh, that's been there all year," Sara piped up. "We've been praying every day you'd come back home, and we wanted to be ready when you did."

Connie summoned the helpers to follow her upstairs, leaving Pete behind. Not knowing what to do, or how to feel, Mai began transferring items from boxes to the empty dresser. Pete joined in, folding baby clothes into the top drawer.

"I'm glad you're back home," he finally said without looking up.

"I'm glad too - - I think. It just feels so strange to be here again." Mai tossed an empty box aside. "I never should have left."

"Well, that's old news. The important thing is, you're back."

"I realize now, you and Mom were just trying to make me into a good person, but I always felt like you were hard on me. I didn't know if that was because I was the oldest, or because I was adopted."

"Oh, MaiLy," Pete sighed. "It was neither. And we weren't trying to make you into a good person - - you already were a good person." He put his face close to hers. "And you still are."

"Well, for a good person, I've made some really bad mistakes." She managed a smile.

"We all make mistakes. It's how we grow from them that counts." He hugged her. "Now that you're home, you'll just keep growing and things will get better and better. You'll see."

"Thanks, Dad." She clung to him. "You rescued me again."

"That was my life-long vow," he said seriously. He went back to stacking clothes in a drawer. "Mom and I want to make this basement into a little apartment for you, so you and Rudy have your own little place here with us." He glanced at the dumbfounded look on Mai's face and quickly added, "But we can talk about that another time."

Connie tiptoed into the room with Rudy sleeping on her shoulder. He was in a new pair of pajamas Mai had never seen before. Grandma Connie placed him in the crib and covered him with a light quilt. They took turns bending over the rail and kissing him on the cheek.

Then Connie kissed Mai. "Better get some sleep, Sweetie. Tomorrow's Saturday. We'll have plenty of time to talk and make plans for you then."

Her old Mickey Mouse night-light dimly illuminated the room. As she lay watching Rudy nestled under his blanket, Mai longed for the peace that calmed his breathing and blessed his sleep.

CHAPTER 36

Mai woke too early, but deliberately lingered in the basement until breakfast was long finished. When she thought she heard rumblings of a family meeting above her, she dawdled even longer. She bathed Rudy in the guest bathroom and dressed him in his Oshkosh overalls and high tops. He giggled as she repeated her daily drill, "Say Mama."

By the time she went upstairs, the breakfast dishes were done and the entire family was in the flurry of completing Saturday chores. She and Rudy finished the leftover oatmeal while David mopped the kitchen floor and Nathan carried out the trash. Mai felt ill at ease and awkward; like an intruder, unsure of her role now.

Before long the activity centered in the basement.

"We're moving all our toys and junk to our own rooms," Sara explained.

"And putting the TV and Nintendo in the family room upstairs," David said. "You get the little TV from Mom and Dad's bedroom."

"Then you and Rudy can live down here," Sara said, then added the obviously rehearsed, "and we'll leave you alone as much as you want."

Soon, Nathan was vacuuming the shag carpet while Elizabeth frantically collected Legos from his path. "We're a family and we all work together," she quoted.

By mid-afternoon, the project was complete. Pete took David and Nathan to soccer practice. Connie taxied Sara and Elizabeth to a Girl Scout cookie sales meeting. Marcie and Erica met friends at the mall. Rudy took a nap.

Mai sat alone in the basement.

By the end of the week, Pete had picked up the rest of Mai's things from Lucy and Joe's and moved them into her quarters.

Connie had brought carpet swatches for Mai to choose from to redecorate the basement.

Ray had called four times begging Mai to come "home".

And the FBI came by to report Maxwell Murphy had been arrested and all charges had been dropped against her.

Connie and Pete found Mai alone on the porch swing Sunday afternoon. They sat beside her and chatted about the greening of the grass and the smell of the lilac blossoms.

Finally, Pete patted Mai's arm and said, "So how are you doing after a week in the family zoo?"

"Pretty good." Mai faked a smile.

"How does it feel to be home again?" A mom question.

"Fine." Then Mai added honestly, "Actually, it feels pretty weird. As glad as I am to be here, I still feel like somehow I don't belong."

"How's that?" Pete asked.

"I still feel different. Like I don't fit in." Mai shrugged. "Geez, that's what I said when I was sixteen."

"But when you were sixteen you tried to show us that by looking different," Pete chuckled. "Remember that spiked hair and black make-up?"

"Yeh. I was trying to 'find myself' - - trying to figure out who I was." Mai grinned and shook her head.

"All adolescents do that," Connie said. "As they start to change, they all ask 'Who am I?' and 'What am I going to do with my life.' It's harder, sometimes, for adopted kids because they feel like they can't figure out their future until they know their past."

"That's it," Mai said.

"It's tougher in cases like yours where there are no records of their pasts to answer those questions."

"I'm sure you're right. I wish I'd listened to you a long time ago, Mom."

"Well, I'm still learning, too." Connie smiled. "The more I work with adoptions, the more I learn how complicated it can be for kids. A lot of it's about control. Sometimes adopted kids think their lives have been managed, or mismanaged, by adults who gave them away then, or boss them around now. So the kid wants to take control. Sometimes she runs away to do that."

"Well, I sure haven't been controlling things very good so far."

Pete put his arm around her. "That's why you're here, Sweetie. We want to help you get control of your life."

Mai spent the next week in her favorite job - - homemaker. While the family was away at work and school, she cared for Rudy and did most of the shopping and cooking. Her days were long and happy, yet she still felt like something was missing - - there was an unexplainable hole in her life. Connie had said most adoptees feel that way at some point, and some try to fill that hole with unhealthy things - - like drugs, or alcohol, or food, or bad relationships. "I've already done all that," Mai muttered as she lifted Rudy from the highchair. "Never again."

Another thing Connie mentioned bothered Mai for several days. She had explained that sometimes-teenage girls take on the identity of their birth mother. Was that why Mai had chosen to live in such poor conditions? Was that why she allowed herself to become pregnant? And is that why her son didn't have a father now?

She wiped pureed pears from Rudy's face, recalling the phone conversation with Ray the day before. Shortly after a dozen long stem roses were delivered, Ray had called to be sure she'd gotten them and the attached love letter. Even though he had misspelled words like "fer-ever" and "new leef," Mai was touched by the sorrow and love he expressed.

On the phone he told her he had been cleared of any involvement in the fraudulent check-cashing scheme. His parole officer approved of his family's plan to move to Las Vegas and start a new life. Ray repeated his love for her and his son and begged her to join them.

"You're all I want in the world, MaiLy," he said. "Let me spend the rest of my life proving to you how much I love you. Think of Rudy," he persisted. "Our son deserves a father - - like you never had when you were a baby. You swore you'd never let that happen to him."

Rudy wrinkled his nose as Mai finished cleaning the lunch off his face before naptime. The rocking chair squeaked in time with the lullaby she hummed. Then she whispered, "I love you, Son. For you, I'm going to be strong and take control of my life."

CHAPTER 37

Pete removed the pushpin and letter from the basement door.

He slumped to the floor and read:

Dear Mom and Dad,

As you know I've been so mixed up lately. I am so confused. I don't know who I am and what I am going to do with my life. You have all been so wonderful to me. I don't deserve all the love and support you give me. Nobody complains, but I know I'm in the way here. You've got more kids to raise. You shouldn't have to be concerned about me and Rudy. If I leave, you won't have to worry about us anymore.

I'm taking control of my life. Starting over. Ray has really changed this time. I'm going to Las Vegas with him and his family. There we can make some good money and Rudy will have a mom and a dad.

I really do love you,

MaiLy

The casino lights flashed in colorful exhilaration against the predawn sky.

"Wow!" Mai rolled down the rental truck window to see the three-story dazzling cowboy waving them to their new home, their new hope. The scintillating miles of sparkling bulbs pulsed excitement through them.

"This is it, Mai!" Ray drummed the steering wheel. "I can feel it! We're going to make it here - - make it big!" He reached over Rudy, asleep in his car seat, and kissed her hard.

They had driven straight through from Denver, towing Mai's car behind. Lucy and Joe had left with the girls two weeks before school was out to find a house for all of them. The money from the sale of their Denver home made a down payment on a similar place in Las Vegas. Mai was surprised anyone would want their old house by the tracks, but they had, in fact, had a couple offers from neighbors. Lucy said she knew all along they were sitting on a gold mine and credited her foresight and good financial planning for this windfall.

"We'll need more to live on, though, until we all find jobs," she had said to Mai before they left. "You must have money stuck away somewhere. I know how much you made and you ain't been spending it all."

Reluctantly, Mai divulged her savings account balance.

"If I'm going to sink everything we have in the world into our new house, the least you can do is chip in 'til we all get on our feet," Lucy admonished.

Mai knew she was right and felt it was only fair to close the account and turn the funds over to Lucy.

"Soon we'll have our own place," Ray promised. "I can get a job with decent pay, then double it at the black-jack tables."

"I don't know," Mai worried. "What if you lose?"

"Trust me," Ray bragged. "What do you think I did all those months in prison? I told you I learned a lot there."

The rising sun dimmed the brilliance as they left the downtown area and pulled into their new neighborhood. They drove by rows of houses, all needing paint and lawn care.

"Here it is. Fifteen-fourteen." Mai tried to hide the disappointment in her voice. The whitewashed siding faded further against the blistered turquoise trim. Grass missing from the bare spots in the lawn seemed to flourish in cracks in the sidewalks and driveway.

"Ma said it was a fixer-upper," Ray offered.

"Ya, but who's going to fix it?" Mai muttered.

She was surprised when Lucy met them at the door, as she was never up this early. She reached for Rudy. "Here, let Grandma take care of Rudy while the rest of you unload the truck."

Without rest, the moving and the settling in began. Rosie and Nicole pitched in and Joe followed Lucy's commands while she supervised the crew.

As they hauled their double bed down the hall, Ray winked at Mai. "At least we have our own room now."

Mai sighed. "And nothing else to put in it." She hadn't had the heart or the courage to return to her parents' house and retrieve the rest of her belongings. Though she was afraid they would contact her after she left, she was disappointed when they didn't. Silently she vowed to write them soon and tell them how well she and Rudy were doing.

By the end of the day, things were mostly in place and, to Mai's surprise, looked better than she expected. The throw covers and decorations from their apartment dressed up the dingy walls and shabby carpet. Joe left to return the rental truck at noon and came home at suppertime with a bucket of chicken and $27.50 in nickels.

"Let's go!" Ray exclaimed to Mai.

"Tonight? No way," Mai said. "We haven't slept in two days. You were complaining earlier how tired you were.

Let's get some sleep tonight, then we can look for jobs, and play tomorrow."

"I'm ready to play now!"

"We've hardly seen Rudy all day," Mai coaxed. "Let's play with him tonight, and go out tomorrow."

"Suit yourself," Ray said as he grabbed a piece of chicken and headed out the door.

Mai fell into an exhausted slumber and didn't hear him come home until he shook her shoulder.

"MaiLy!" Ray said in a loud whisper.

"You've been drinking," she groaned and rolled away from him.

"Only a little. They give it to you free when you gamble! Anyway, that's not the point. Look at this!" He waved a fist full of bills in her face. "Look at this! It was so easy!"

Mai turned toward him, rubbed her eyes, and watched as he thumbed a wad of cash.

"That's great, Ray," she muttered, and rolled over again.

"It WAS great!" He paced around the room. Rudy fussed in the crib beside them. "And it will BE great," Ray whispered as he shed his clothes and crawled into bed. His hands groped her thighs and hips.

"Ray, I'm too tired," she murmured.

"That's okay," he breathed in her ear. "I'm excited enough for both of us."

The sun shone through the grimy bedroom window. *My next project,* Mai thought as her eyes peeped open, *will be washing windows.* Ray came in wearing only a towel secured at his waist. He removed it and began drying his shoulder length hair.

"Up and at 'em, little Mama," he said, snapping the towel in Mai's direction. "We have a big day ahead. People to see, things to do, jobs to find, games to play." He pounced onto the bed beside her and pulled back her covers. "Unless you just want to stay in bed and play."

Mai hopped out the other side. "Then we'd better get started," she said smiling and grabbing her robe. "This is a big day for us."

Everyone at the breakfast table shared the same enthusiasm, except for Nicole. When she learned she had to baby sit Rudy and Rosie while everyone else went job-hunting, the mood suddenly changed.

"Why do I have to stay home with them? I'm almost sixteen. I can get a job."

"Doing what?" Lucy scoffed. "Look at you!"

Nicole had dyed her hair black before they left Denver. Her bright red lipstick contrasted boldly against her pasty white makeup. Always dressed in black, she wore several chain bracelets and three pierced hoops in each ear.

"What's wrong with how I look?"

Her family answered with boisterous laughter. Nicole stormed out of the kitchen and slammed the door to her room behind her. Mai tapped gently on the door and offered to talk, but Nicole didn't respond. Any closeness she and Mai had developed over the years was deteriorating as Nicole withdrew from the family. Mai's belief that she could still positively affect Nicole's life was a major factor in her decision to join them in Las Vegas. And, it seemed, Nicole's love for Rudy was one of the few motivating factors in her life.

Mai dressed in a cotton skirt and blouse and twisted her long hair atop her head. She wore little makeup these days, but smoothed a dab of blush on her high cheekbones. It took a lot of convincing for Ray to wear the khaki pants she had bought him instead of his faded blue jeans. Because exploring casinos was his first priority, they agreed to have fun in the morning and job hunt in the afternoon.

They parked in a lot behind the Circus Circus Casino and walked The Strip. Though daylight dimmed the sensational brilliance, Mai sensed an electrifying excitement looming.

"Wait 'til you see this place after dark!" Ray beamed, so proud of last night's discoveries.

Mai remembered the Riviera mentioned on old TV shows and was eager to go there first. Inside, a chorus of a thousand clanging slot machines greeted them. Mai gawked at plush red carpets and ornate chandeliers. "I feel like I'm in another world," she said as Ray led her toward the noise.

He pulled a wad of cash from his pocket and handed it to the woman pushing a change cart. Then he gave Mai two rolls of nickels and suggested she sit next to him and watch. Repeatedly, he dropped nickels into the slot and pulled the lever.

"You try," he said without breaking rhythm.

Mai followed his technique and grinned, watching rows of fruit spin before her. When her roll was half gone, the machine chimed, "Ting, ting, ting, ting," and hundreds of nickels clattered into the tray.

"I won!" she screamed to the obvious amusement of fellow gamblers.

"Thirty-seven dollars!" Ray said, scooping the change into paper cups.

"Now what do I do with it?"

"Put it back in," Ray coached. "That's how you make more money."

"I don't know. This will buy a lot of groceries."

"That's not how you gamble, MaiLy."

"Okay," she said and then, one by one, emptied her cups.

"I should have kept it," she pouted.

The lady next to her puffed from her cigarette. "That's why they call it the one-armed-bandit, Honey."

"Don't be so disappointed," Ray said. "There's plenty more where that came from. Let's try someplace else."

At the Stardust they feasted at the bountiful all-you-can-eat buffet and went, again, to the slot machines. Mai winced when Ray bought rolls of quarters instead of nickels.

"You got to spend big to win big," he said. When his roll was gone he decided this place wasn't lucky for him, and they headed to Circus Circus.

As they walked in the sunshine, Mai marveled at seeing palm trees again. They seemed like long-lost friends waving a new promise. Hand in hand, she and Ray strolled past rows of wedding chapels.

"Maybe we can get married here, Mai."

She didn't answer.

He gestured to an Elvis impersonator standing in front of a tiny white chapel with a steeple. "Maybe Elvis can marry us!" He laughed. Then pointing across the street he added, "Or maybe we'll just keep it simple and have a drive through wedding someday."

"Maybe someday," Mai said.

A man was handing out fliers on the sidewalk and stuffed one in Mai's hand as she passed. She thanked him politely and read the hot pink sheet as they ambled on.

She stopped. "They're selling sex!" she gasped, then dropped the paper as if it were on fire.

Ray laughed. "It's legal here."

Mai noticed a church's cross towering behind a casino. "What kind of a place is this?"

Circus Circus reminded her of the fun she had as a little girl when her family went to Elitch Gardens amusement park. She and her brother and sisters spent most of their allowances on the midway there, winning tiny trinkets instead of the mammoth stuffed animals used as bait. Instead of her daddy, now Ray threw balls at milk bottles and shotguns at targets to win her the big prize. Mai cheered him on and Ray took a deep bow when arcade lights flashed and whistled announcing his win. He presented Mai with a three-foot trophy disguised as a white plush baboon. They sat munching popcorn and kissing and hugging as the high-wire act performed in the high top.

Then, whirring lights and spewing coins lured them back to the casino where they were mentored at the roulette wheel. Mai nervously placed a dollar on black and odd while Ray made his way to a nearby blackjack table. The roulette wheel spun and the little ball bounced. When it finally stopped the young blonde woman next to Mai said, "You won."

"I did?" Mai giggled. She continued to bet on black and odd and continued to win until her one dollar had become twenty-five. Mai felt guilty when she noticed the man next to her was losing 100-dollar bets each time she won.

The blonde engaged her in fun conversation, as if gambling was their common bond of friendship.

"It's easier if you think of it as 'tokens' instead of money," she offered with a laugh. "At home I clip coupons for Cheerios, and here I drop a week's grocery allowance in a minute."

Twice, a waitress in net stockings and a feathery leotard asked Mai if she wanted a drink. Mai declined.

Before long, Mai's twenty-five dollar profit grew to forty. "I'll stop at fifty," she told her new friend.

"Black and odd seems to work for you!" the blonde said. "Why did you pick that?"

"It describes my features best," Mai laughed.

When the forty turned to fifty, Mai vowed to stop at seventy-five.

When it reached seventy-five, she swore she'd quit at one hundred.

And she did.

As she gathered up her chips, Ray returned. His breath and demeanor made it clear he had not declined the free drinks. When he saw her winnings, Ray kissed her and twirled her in his arms. "See? I told you it would be great here!"

LeAnn Thieman

It took a lot of persuading for him to keep their agreement to look for jobs that afternoon. Grudgingly, he accompanied Mai to personnel offices in several casinos where they completed application forms and, on two occasions, five-minute interviews. Ray lied about his past work experiences and, of course, his criminal record.

"It's a fresh start, Mai," he said in his defense. "I can't let my past spoil our future."

Reluctantly, they headed home at suppertime as planned. Nicole had made sandwiches and was feeding Rudy in the high chair when they gathered at the table. Lucy and Joe told tales of success at the crap tables but failure in the job search. Mai's one hundred dollar win topped all other stories.

Lucy plunked a battered coffee canister on the table. "Let's all put all our winnings in here so we can share them."

Slowly, Mai placed her money in the can.

"It's only fair," Lucy said.

The next day Mai stayed home with Rudy while the rest of the family went to Circus Circus. As much as she had enjoyed the day before, she was happy to spend the day with her son. She took him for a morning walk in his stroller, but he insisted on pushing it the last block home. She guided it by the handle as he marched proudly behind it, his face barely peeking over the seat back. His big smile wrinkled his nose and made his chubby cheeks crowd his squinting eyes. His dark brown eyes and black hair reminded Mai of herself. "He's a little me!" she had said to her folks when he was born. Then to herself she had said, "and I will give you all I never had. I promise."

Their walk confirmed her suspicions that the adjoining neighborhoods were as run down as theirs. "Soon I will give you a better home," she pledged as she carried Rudy into the house. "I promise."

She read him his favorite *Green Eggs and Ham* and *Hand, Hand, Fingers, Thumb* as they cuddled in the rocker.

218

He patted her cheeks and gave her a slobbery kiss before she tucked him in for a nap. Then she began her window-washing project.

That's when the personnel manager from the Riviera called offering her a position selling change. Her grocery store experience handling large amounts of money qualified her for the job, and her former employer had given her an excellent recommendation. *That's the least he can do,* Mai thought, *since he falsely accused me of a crime.* She would begin on the graveyard shift, but that was fine with Mai. Then she'd have daytimes with Rudy. Training on the day shift would start tomorrow, and her new position would begin in a week. The pay and benefits were better than she expected. Soon she and Ray could get a place of their own.

Excitedly, Mai told the rest of the family about her new job when they returned for the supper she had prepared. It was decided Nicole would watch Rudy while Mai slept during the day. Meanwhile, the others would keep looking for work.

Within a month a routine was established. Ray got a day job washing dishes at the Riviera. He was supposed to be home evenings to spend time with his wife and son, but that rarely happened. After working hard all day he needed time to unwind, he claimed, and usually arrived home in time for Mai to take the car to work at 11:00. He kept his promise not to drink too much so he could hear Rudy if he needed him in the night.

Mai enjoyed her job and interacting with all the people. Her coworkers were supportive and friendly, especially Sharon, a happily married mom who worked Mai's shift. Already they had shared breaks and life stories.

Exhausted, Mai stumbled into the house most mornings about 8:00. Rudy's smile re-energized her through feeding him breakfast. Then she fell into bed until Nicole banged on her bedroom door at exactly 2:00 p.m.

By the end of summer, Mai was a little uneasy, wondering how much attention Nicole was giving Rudy.

Occasionally, as she slept, Mai heard him fussing for an unusually long time. She would stagger to the living room to find Nicole engrossed in a soap opera and Rudy in the playpen. When she shared these concerns with Ray, he convinced her she was over reacting.

One morning, in late July, Mai woke to Rudy's cough. When his hacking turned to gagging, she flung back the covers and bolted to the living room.

Rudy was alone, sitting in the playpen with a bag of potato chips beside him.

His face reddened as he wheezed and sputtered. With terror in his teary eyes, he gasped for breath and began turning blue. Mai heard herself scream as she grabbed him and, remembering her first aid training in baby sitting class, turned him over her lap and pounded his back.

His body grew limp. His gasping faint.

"Please God!" Mai prayed as she struck him repeatedly between the shoulder blades. With a final cough, a potato chip ejected to the floor and Rudy let out a terrified cry. Kissing his sweaty face, she rocked him in her shaking arms. Together they cried softly, consoling each other.

The front door stood open and Mai carried him to the step. From there she could see Nicole talking to a boy at the end of the block.

"No more," she said, then carried her son to her bedroom and packed.

CHAPTER 38

By the time Sharon arrived in her Datsun pickup, Mai had her suitcase and several boxes overflowing on the front step. When the cartons she had stowed under the bed were full, she ripped the throws off the living room couch and chair and bundled more clothes and belongings in them. In the kitchen, she packed all the dishes she'd bought while working in the grocery store.

Nicole had come in, but stormed out again, yelling something about none of this being her fault.

With Sharon's help, Mai disassembled the bunk beds and loaded them in the truck. Then the high chair, the playpen, and the creaky rocker she'd bought at the flea market. She took the color TV she'd purchased on time payments, but left the stereo system. That had been a gift to Joe.

Tears rolled down her cheeks as she took photos of Rudy off the wall. She'd gotten them at Sears when she still had her secret savings account.

"You okay?" Sharon asked.

221

Mai held the framed photo to her chest. "Yes. First I felt furious, now I just feel free." With that, she snatched up a laundry basket and headed to the bathroom where she collected all the linen she'd paid for over the years. She went back to Nicole's closet to retrieve all the clothes she had loaned her, but decided to leave them instead.

"I called Ray at work," Sharon said. "I told him not to drive home, but to meet us at my house. I said we'd explain later."

"Thanks, Sharon. You're such a good friend. I don't know what I'd do without you now."

"Well, you can have the kids' bedroom for a night or two. They'll love camping on the living room floor. We can park the truck in our garage for a couple days until you find another place." She put her arm around Mai's shoulder. "Our old apartment complex rents from month to month and always has openings. It isn't much nicer than this, I'm afraid, so you won't want to be there long. But at least it will get you out of here."

Mai looked around at the ransacked house. "I think I have everything," she said as she closed cupboard doors and straightened the throw rug.

Sharon said softly, "I'll take Rudy to the truck and get him settled in the our car seat. Come on out when you're ready."

Sharon left. Mai took a deep breath. "I'm ready."

Heading for the door, she paused, then went back to the kitchen and took the battered coffee canister from its hiding place. Opening it, she realized she had been the only one putting money in it. She dumped the cash into her purse and left the open canister setting empty in the middle of the table next to her house key.

Pulling the front door closed behind her, she skipped down the steps. Sharon looked puzzled as Mai kicked off her sandals and ran barefoot to the truck.

CHAPTER 39

"I can't believe you did this!" Ray shouted. "All my life I wanted to leave them like this, but didn't have the guts." He waved his arm around their barren apartment. "This is gonna be great."

"It's going to be hard," Mai said as he hugged her. "It took both our paychecks for the deposit and first month's rent. We have to live on the coffee can money for the rest of the month."

"Oh, I can win more," Ray said.

"No, Ray. We can't gamble this. We can't risk losing it. Besides, you're not going to have much time to 'unwind' after work anymore." They shoved the bunk beds together and put a double sheet over them. "I'll get home in the mornings in time for you to go to work at eight. Then I'll stay up all day and take care of Rudy. I'll nap when he does. But you'll need to come right home after work at 4:00. We'll have an early supper together, then I'll have to sleep from six until ten or so while you watch Rudy."

"I can do that."

"You have to, Ray. It's the only way we can do this." She hugged him again. "We're a family, and we all work together."

Ray kissed her. "We'll be fine. I promise."

And for the next few months, things were fine. They bought a used kitchen table and returned the borrowed card table and chairs to Sharon. She sold them the old couch from her basement for twenty dollars, insisting she was just going to give it to Good Will anyway.

Ray came home promptly after work and they spent an hour or so loving and laughing and playing with Rudy. She usually gave Rudy his bath and got him ready for bed before she went to sleep. She loved that task and Ray seemed to find it annoying.

Occasionally they left Rudy with Mrs. Kralik next door while they went out together. The grandmotherly woman had brought them homemade bread the day they moved in and offered to baby sit Rudy for short periods. On her days off, Mai took her shopping and loved spending long mornings listening to the old woman's legends. Mrs. Kralik adored Rudy and radiated a youthful glow when she was with him.

"I'll watch the baby," she'd say. "It's important that the two of you keep dating. My husband Ralph and I, God rest his soul, went dancing every week. That's what keeps you young and in love."

She claimed she was living in this apartment temporarily - - only until her son came for her. Another neighbor told Mai she'd been saying that for three years.

Mai and Ray bought a "Charlie Brown Christmas tree" and decorated it with strands of popcorn and cranberries, like Mai had done at home. She sent her Denver family a Christmas card and the Sears photo of Rudy. She longed to call them and ached to hear their voices, but for reasons she still couldn't explain, she wouldn't allow herself that joy. She and Ray didn't have a phone, so her parents couldn't call her, either. Still, they sent a huge box filled with presents and family photos.

Lucy and Joe didn't contact them over Christmas. They had stopped by the casino only once since Mai left, and berated her for taking items the family was sharing. Their insults and profanity upset Mai so; she vowed never to be with them again. Ray took Rudy to their home a few times, but even those visits were rare.

Mai baked a small turkey breast and prepared store-bought stuffing and cranberries. A green bed sheet served as a tablecloth as they celebrated their first Christmas alone.

They had agreed to buy inexpensive gifts for each other, so Mai was stunned when she opened a necklace from Ray. "These look like real diamonds!" she gasped.

"They are! I saved some money on the side to surprise you," he said.

Her worry about how he acquired it overrode her joy in receiving it.

The next week, he brought home a five-piece component stereo system. When she subtly asked where he got the money, Ray became enraged. He yelled about trust and love and trying to turn over a new leaf. Punching his fist through the closet door, he bellowed about not being appreciated. He shoved Mai into the wall and stormed out of the apartment.

When he returned a few hours later, he said ruefully, "I'm sorry I pushed you, Mai."

"It was my fault, too, Ray," she said. "I shouldn't have doubted you when you've worked so hard to change."

Then he made rough love to her on the couch, as if sex were the ultimate apology.

When he didn't show up for work on New Year's Eve, Mai's stifled doubts were unleashed.

He was gone for two days, then came home, drunk.

After he sobered up the next day, he acted as if nothing happened.

"My first husband used to do that," Mrs. Kralik said when she babysat Rudy on short notice. "Sometimes he just needed to go on a binge, then he'd be fine for a long time again."

And Ray was fine for several months. He came home right after work and brought Mai flowers at least once a week. He doted on Rudy more than ever before and on his second birthday bought him a miniature bat, ball, and glove. Mai's parents had sent Rudy the same thing, but she hid those gifts before Ray saw them.

When Mai's supervisor called her into his office for her annual review, she expected a reprimand for arriving late for work while Ray was on his binge. She was flabbergasted when, instead, he gave her an excellent review, a raise, and a promotion.

"You've been an outstanding employee, MaiLy," he said. "Sharon tells me things aren't always easy at home, yet your performance here is exemplary. I'd like you to take the position as a Keno runner on the evening shift. The base pay is higher and the tips substantial. A woman with your kindness and gracious charm could make a good living."

Mai's head was spinning when she left his office.

Ray's first reaction surprised her. "Have you seen what they wear? Low cut, skimpy outfits with black tights. And do you see the way men look at them?" But when he heard about the increased pay, he had only positive things to say about the promotion.

Mrs. Kralik was delighted to watch Rudy from 3:00 when Mai went to work until Ray got home at 4:00.

"Then you'll have a whole evening taking care of Rudy by yourself, Ray," Mai said. "Will you be okay with that until I get home at midnight?"

"Of course I'll be okay," Ray snapped. "Don't you think I can take care of my own son?"

He did take good care of Rudy for several weeks. Then Mrs. Kralik called Mai at work at 6:00 to say Ray hadn't picked up Rudy yet.

"I got tied up at work," Ray hollered when Mai asked for an explanation.

Sometimes Mai came home at midnight to find Rudy in his crib, sleeping in the same clothes he'd worn all day. When she found him asleep on the living room floor, his face and clothes still smeared with supper, Mai woke Ray, snoring on the couch.

"Why didn't you take care of him?" she accused, shaking Ray's shoulder. He slapped her hand away, so she shook him again. "Why didn't you take care of him?" This time his wallop sent her sailing backward over the coffee table.

Rudy woke, screaming, "Mama! Mama!" She picked him up and rushed into the bathroom, locking the door behind them. As she gently washed Rudy's tear-streaked face, Ray beat at the door.

"You think you can do better? You think you can do this without me? Go ahead and try!" The apartment door slammed so hard the pictures rattled on the wall.

She changed Rudy into his pajamas and rocked him in the creaky rocker until they both stopped crying.

"I'm so sorry, MaiLy," Ray said, the bouquet trembling in his hand. "I didn't mean to hurt you. You just surprised me, is all."

"I'm sorry, too, Ray. I shouldn't have shook you that way and scared you."

He started coming home on time every day. Rudy was always bathed, in his pajamas, and in bed when Mai got home. Ray played ball with Rudy and gloated when he taught him to say, "I'm Daddy's boy." He brought Mai diamond earrings to match her necklace.

When Sharon noticed a bruise on Mai's arm a few months later, Mai said she bumped it moving furniture.

Sharon persisted. "Those look like finger marks, MaiLy."

Mai finally admitted Ray had grabbed her arm when they argued the day before. "It's as much my fault as his," Mai said. "I nag him too much. I had it coming."

"No woman has abuse coming," Sharon said.

Mai fired back. "I'm not abused! I should know better than to confront him when he's drinking."

Sharon stroked Mai's bruised arm. "If you ever need anything, day or night, I'm here." Before leaving the break room she added, "You deserve better, MaiLy."

"I wonder."

The next day was Ray's day off so he agreed to watch Rudy while Mai shopped for groceries. When she came home, Rudy and Ray weren't there. She knocked on Mrs. Kralik's door to see if she had seen them.

"He was drinkin'," she said in a loud whisper, as if someone in the hall might hear. "I said I'd watch Rudy, but he said he could take care of his own son, thank you very much." She leaned closer to Mai. "I don't mean to pry, Honey, but you got trouble there. That boy is no good. I hear what goes on over there. His drinkin' is the problem. If you ask me, I'd say it's time to leave him."

Mai stood, staring at her. "You said yourself some men need to go on binges sometimes - - even your first husband."

"That's why I got a second husband," Mrs. Kralik said softly, and closed the door.

Mai ran frantically through the halls of the apartment complex, and raced outside to look around the building. Gray clouds rumbled, releasing a gentle rain. In the back parking lot, she found Ray sitting with Rudy on his knee on the bottom step of the fire escape - - an empty six pack beside them.

"What are you doing?" Mai yelled.

"Me and my son are just having a little man-to-man talk," he said, swigging from another bottle. "No women allowed." Ray stood and Rudy fell from his lap onto the muddy ground and cried. Ray reached for him, but swerved into the rail instead.

Mai swept Rudy into her arms and ran to the car. Her hands shook so; she could barely get the key in the ignition.

"No more, son. No more."

The seven-story cross, had stood waiting in the background like a quiet loyal friend. Mai saw it on her way to work each day, ignoring its reminder- -*I'm here whenever you need me - - whenever you're ready.*

In the rain, she held Rudy in one arm and with the other, pulled the heavy hand-carved wooden door open. She hesitated in the back of the empty church, wondering if she belonged there. Her footsteps echoed in the stillness as she drifted toward the front, her eyes fixed on a magnificent mural of the Risen Christ there.

She slid into a wooden pew and gazed up at the stained glass window depicting Jesus consoling his mother as he carried the cross. Rumbling thunder sent a chill through Mai's already trembling body.

She stood Rudy on the seat beside her and knelt; back straight, hands folded, fingertips pointed up.

"Dear God," she started, then draped herself over the pew and sobbed. Gasping between mournful wails, all the grief and fear harbored all those years, poured out. Another crash of thunder reeled her back to the night she ran, through the bombing, from the orphanage. She could see the soldier who lay bleeding to death in her path. *That's how I feel,* she thought.

Rudy whimpered quietly beside her.

"What should I do? Show me the way, Lord. Give me some sign of hope." She rested her head in her folded arms, unable to stop the tears.

She felt Rudy gently pat her back. "Be okay, Mama."

Mai raised her head and saw him smiling weakly.

That's when a sunbeam streamed through the stained glass window, filling the hollow emptiness with a warm glow.

Ray wasn't in the apartment when she got back.

Mai started throwing clothes in the suitcase and boxes she'd saved. She dumped entire dresser drawers into a carton while Rudy stood staring.

"It's okay, Buddy," she said. "We're getting out of here. You - - we- - deserve better."

As she yanked an armload of clothes off their hangers, she heard Ray come in. He shoved Rudy aside. "Get out of the way!" He grabbed Mai by her hair and flung her to the carpet.

"Ray! Stop!"

With both hands, he dragged her by the hair, onto the bed. "Where do you think you're going?"

Mai recoiled her legs and kicked them into his chest, hurling him into the wall. He staggered, stunned, with clumps of her hair still in his fists. He fell to his knees, bawling. "Don't leave me, MaiLy. I beg you, don't leave me."

"Daddy!" Rudy cried. Then to Mai, "Mommy!"

"It's okay, son," she said picking him up.

She grabbed the suitcase and headed for the door. Ray rummaged madly under the bed.

"MaiLy!" he screamed.

She turned.

Ray held a pistol to his temple.

She almost dropped Rudy. "Where'd you get that?"

"Same place I got your necklace, earrings, stereo - - I stole it. For years I hoped the cops would kill me, and they didn't. So now I'll kill myself. I swear, MaiLy, if you walk out that door, I'll pull this trigger! I'll end my pathetic life!"

Mai stared at the tears on his cheeks, the sorrow in his eyes, the finger on the trigger. She said, "What you do with your life is up to you, Ray," and she walked out.

CHAPTER 40

Her new apartment was on a beautiful street near a park. Sunshine filled the room and Mai's heart as she unpacked her grocery store dishes into the cupboard. She and Rudy had stayed at Sharon's only a few days before Mai found this tiny efficiency apartment. She would have to be frugal to afford it, but she was used to that.

Thanks to Sharon and her husband, John, Mai got her entire damage deposit back. When they helped her move, they stayed to scour the place cleaner than Mai had found it. John had come along mostly as protection in case Ray showed up. When Mai filed the restraining order against him, the police reminded her to still be cautious. As John fixed the hole in the closet door, Mai ached with pity for Ray. She wondered daily how he was doing, but then banished those thoughts from her mind.

Sharon unwrapped more dishes from the packing paper and handed them to Mai. "I know a college student who can baby sit Rudy here in the evenings while you work."

"I'm afraid to leave him with anyone any more," Mai sighed.

"That's pretty understandable," Sharon said. "It may take awhile for you to learn to trust people again."

As the months passed, Mai settled into a happy, though hectic, routine. Gail was, indeed, an ideal baby sitter. She researched activities three-year-olds liked, and brought a new bag of toys and learning tools each week. Because she was about Mai's age, they also became friends. Sometimes she spent her free time with Mai and Rudy, playing at the park or satisfying her insatiable appetite for ice cream.

"I feel like I finally have control of my own life," Mai said one day over a double dip of butter pecan at Baskin Robbins. "I don't know why it took me so long."

Rudy sat in a booster seat licking his Rocky Road.

"I have total responsibility for my son and my own life now, Gail, and I love it." Mai licked her cone absentmindedly. " I had a few sessions with the counselor Sharon recommended. It's a lot easier now to see how I got everything so messed up in my life."

"Hindsight is always pretty clear," Gail said. "You're a strong woman, Mai. It took a lot of courage to leave Ray and his family."

"It wasn't easy, and still isn't some days," Mai said as she mopped the brown puddle dripping from Rudy's elbows. "I pray to God every day for the strength to keep it up."

The following week, as Mai carried her Keno tray through the Riviera lounge, a familiar voice called, "MaiLy?"

"Lucy. Joe. What are you doing here?"

"We need your help."

Mai walked passed them. "I can't talk now. I have to work."

"Ray needs you."

Mai stopped and turned to face them. "Is he okay?"

"He's in big trouble this time. Armed robbery. A parole violation. Seems he didn't have things cleared to leave Colorado after all, so this time they're throwing the book at him."

"I have nothing left to offer Ray," Mai said firmly. "It's over."

"He needs bail. You at least have money to offer him, don't you? Working at a fancy place like this."

"I gave Ray all I had," Mai said and turned to walk away.

"You going to abandon the father of your child?" Lucy hollered. Patrons stared.

Mai glared back over her shoulder. "Most any man can father a child. It takes a good man to be a dad." Then she walked through the door that said "Employees Only".

Lucy and Joe came back three more times that week, pleading. Lucy wiped pretend tears as she told about Ray sitting in the cell, begging for MaiLy. She went on with tales of Nicole's delinquency and concerns about Rosie following in her sister's wayward footsteps. Mai finally mustered the courage to get a restraining order against them.

She never saw them again.

A month later, at work, she heard another familiar voice call her name. Looking in the mirrored wall, she saw the reflection of her father. She turned, frozen.

Pete opened his arms wide. "Hi, Honey."

She dropped her Keno tray onto the bar. "Dad."

His embrace enveloped her in the love only a parent can bestow. Patrons looked on and smiled as she rocked in her daddy's arms.

Pete took a deep breath, faked a cough, then stood holding her hands.

"I'm in town on business for two days. Do you have time to see me?"

"Perfect," Mai beamed. "I'm off all day tomorrow."

"I know you can't talk now. I'm staying at the Stardust. Call me when you get up in the morning." He gave her another hug. "It's wonderful seeing you. And I can hardly wait to see my grandson."

Pete met them in the park the next noon carrying a picnic lunch and a kite. He approached Rudy slowly and said, "Remember me?"

"Hi, Grandpa!" Rudy waved.

Mai laughed at the astonished look on her dad's face. "I've kept all the pictures you sent setting out where Rudy sees them all the time." She kissed his cheek. "We've been rehearsing this day for a long time."

As they shared the sandwiches, Pete filled Mai in on all the family news. Marcie and Erica were in college and the rest of the kids were busy with school activities and sports. Connie was still a busy mom and traveling more with FVNC as the organization grew, helping more children in more countries.

They threw the trash in the barrel and headed for the swings. With Rudy on his lap, Pete grinned. "This reminds me of old times."

As they swung together, Mai confessed all that had happened since she left Denver. She couldn't face her dad when she related some parts of the story. When she concluded he simply said, "I'm so proud of you."

"Proud of me?" Mai almost laughed.

"You're a survivor, MaiLy. Sure, you've made some bad decisions, but now you're making good ones. You've come through this a stronger, better person."

"Thanks, Dad. I really mean that. Even though I kept leaving you, I never could have done this without you." She kicked at the sand under the swing. "The thing I finally figured out is, nobody will care for me until I care for myself. I was always trying to fix things- - for Ray - - for his family. It took me forever to learn I can't change people and make them something they're not. Finally I learned to take care of me and Rudy first."

"Some people spend their whole lives figuring that out." Pete smiled. "You're way ahead of most."

Rudy jumped down and ran to the sandbox.

"I thank God every day for him," Mai said. "When I found out I was pregnant, I thought it was the worst thing that could happen to me. It turns out it was the best. Without him I wouldn't have found myself."

They watched Rudy make roads in the sand and push an imaginary truck over them while vibrating his lips like an engine.

"I'm sorry I gave you and Mom such a hard time," Mai blurted.

"You don't have to apologize, Honey." Pete reached over and stroked her arm.

"I still don't know what I was rebelling against."

"Most teenagers don't. I call them 'rebels without a clue,'" Pete snickered.

Mai's smiled half-heartedly. "I met with a counselor a few times after I left Ray. I was so mixed up. She said I was dealing with issues of self-esteem," Mai said as if reciting from a text. "Because I devalued myself, I hung around people who were a negative influence - - like that's what I deserved. She said low self-esteem is common with adopted kids."

"Common with lots of teens, adopted or not," Pete interjected.

Mai nodded, remembering all her friends as a teenager.

"She also said a lot of adopted kids unconsciously play the 'will-you-love-me-if' game. They're always testing whether there's something they can do that will make you not love them any more - - especially if they think their birth mother didn't love or want them."

"It's sadly ironic," Pete said. "Adopted kids are probably wanted more than many kids today. Their adoptive parents labor for them as much as the birth mom did."

Rudy ran across the grass dragging the kite on the ground.

Pete jumped up. "Let Grandpa, show you."

Mai convinced Pete a night on her couch would be better than any hotel room. So they spent the rest of the day and into the night recalling every memory. Over pizza and Pepsi on the living room floor, Pete started from the first day he met her at Domani de Marie. When he got to the part about the paddleboat ride, Mai rollicked with laughter.

"I was such a brat!" she howled. "I'm surprised you still wanted to adopt me!"

"I knew you were created to be ours. Nothing would stop me."

After breakfast the next morning, Pete took a camera from his backpack. Mai and Rudy posed for a whole roll of pictures before Pete headed to the airport. As they hugged good-bye, Mai sent her love to the family and promised she would never leave their lives again. They walked arm in arm to the car, and after a final hug, Pete got in and started the engine.

"Come again, Dad, whenever you're in town. I forgot to ask. What business brought you here this time?"

Pete shifted the car into gear and said, "You."

CHAPTER 41

"I think that guy over there likes you," Mai's coworker whispered.

"Sure he does."

"Seriously. Haven't you noticed he's come in here every month or so for the past few years?"

"Lots of businessmen come to Las Vegas regularly."

"But this guy always, I mean always, sits in the area you're working. Haven't you noticed him, MaiLy?"

Mai looked at the handsome young Asian man at the bar. She had noticed him. When things were so bad with Ray, this man's charming smile and brief conversations had cheered her.

"I think he wants to ask you out. He's been asking me lots of questions about you."

"Not interested," Mai said. Several of her friends had arranged dates for her over the past year, and they had all been the same. After complimenting her beauty, they all seemed too eager to explore it. She learned the best way to dampen their interest was to mention how expensive it was supporting her four- year-old son.

As usual, Mai couldn't avoid the handsome man as she made her rounds through the bar.

"Good to see you again, MaiLy," he said as she took his bet. "We've talked off and on for the past year, but never officially met. I'm Ron."

"Nice to meet you, Ron," Mai said politely, trying to stifle her usual charm. Then pretending another customer was summoning her, she scurried away.

Ron continued to come into the lounge two nights a month, every month, for the next year. She began looking forward to their friendly conversations. Yet every visit, he asked her out, and every time, she declined.

"That's okay," he would smile his charming smile. "I'll wait 'til you're ready."

"Why are you so afraid of him?" Gail asked over a double dip of Bananaversery ice cream.

"I'm not afraid of him."

"Then why won't you go out with him? He's asked you often enough."

"I don't know."

Rudy looked up from his Bubble Gum ice cream cone. "She's not interested in pursuing a relationship at this time."

Gail sputtered ice cream down the front of her shirt. "Where does a five-year-old learn this kind of talk?"

"From Mom," Rudy said. "She says it all the time."

"Eat your ice cream, Son," Mai laughed. "Rudy and I are doing just fine, Gail. I don't need a man in my life telling me what to do."

"Not all men tell you what to do, Mai."

"Maybe I just don't want to get close to anyone again. I'm not sure it's worth risking another rejection."

"Ah. Risk. Now there's the key word. You're going to have to risk again to love again, MaiLy."

"I know. Everybody at work thinks we'd be a great couple. I guess there's some assumption that, because he's Asian, we'd be perfect together."

"So are you just trying to defy some racial thing?"

"No. Though the fact that he's Asian worries me some. If he's interested in me because I can share his culture, he'll be disappointed. Maybe he expects me to speak Vietnamese! In spite of what many people may assume, I consider myself All-American."

Rudy's cheeks bulged as he chewed a huge wad of gum from his ice cream. After much spitting and blowing, a pink bubble burst, covering his eyebrows, cheeks and nose.

Gail asked, "What about Bubble Boy here? What's Ron think of him?"

"He says the fact that I have a son is one of the things he finds most attractive about me."

"Is he still sending you roses at work?"

"At least once a month. But he never pushes me. He's always a gentleman. In fact, he gave me his home number in San Francisco. He says he won't ask me out again until I call him. Meanwhile, he'll wait patiently, he says."

"So let me get this straight. This is a wonderful man who happens to be tall, dark, and handsome and very charming. He's a real gentleman, he's happy you have a son, he seems to make a good living, and he's crazy about you, even willing to wait this whole past year for you. Well, I can certainly see why you wouldn't want to take a risk on somebody like that!"

"Eat your ice cream, Gail."

Mai twisted her hair atop her head then let it fall to her shoulders again.

"Which looks better?" she asked Gail and Rudy who were playing checkers on the coffee table. "Up or down?"

"Down," Gail said without looking.

"Gail's right," Rudy said. "Men like long hair."

"Then up it is," Mai said, twisting her locks in a bun on top of her head.

"Mom, why are you freaking out? It's just one date."

"I never should have called him," Mai said, hustling back to the bedroom again. "We were doing just fine being friends."

She reappeared wearing a bulky brown sweater and baggy pants.

Gail looked up this time and smiled. "No matter how hard you try to hide it, you're still very beautiful, MaiLy."

"How come you wouldn't let him pick you up here?" Rudy asked. "I want to meet him, too."

"I'd rather meet him there. I don't want any one getting to know you, until I get to know him first."

Mai kissed her son on the forehead and headed out the door.

When she entered the restaurant, Ron motioned her to their table. He stood, smiling, as she approached, and held her chair as she was seated. Mai noticed theirs was the only table with a single, long stemmed rose.

"I'm glad to see you. I was afraid you wouldn't come."

"I was afraid I wouldn't either," Mai said with half a laugh. "I'm not too crazy about this dating thing."

"Then let's say it's not a date." He smiled and handed her the rose. "Let's just say it's two friends getting to know each other better."

Mai relaxed. "Okay, friend. Tell me about yourself."

"Well, let's see," he said as he poured them each a glass of wine. "Chablis?"

Mai nodded. "My favorite."

"I know." There was that smile again.

"My folks immigrated from Canton, China. I was born and raised in San Francisco's Chinatown. My father owned a business there."

Ron talked on for nearly an hour, about himself and his family of five brothers and sisters. Mai listened, enthralled with the stories, but mostly with Ron's enthusiasm and love in telling them.

"Mom and Dad have continued lots of Chinese traditions, but I consider myself pretty much All-

American," he said as he twirled spaghetti on his fork. "It's always funny when people expect me to speak Chinese instead of English." He took a sip of wine. "Your turn, friend," he said with a wink. "What story would you like to share?"

Mai stirred at the spaghetti on her plate, surprised how at ease and comfortable she felt. "I was adopted when I was ten, and one of my first meals in my new home was spaghetti." When she told of their contest to see who could suck the longest strand without stopping, Ron chuckled. They both tried to keep from laughing too loudly as she described the sauce-smeared faces singing "On Top Of Spaghetti All Covered With Cheese."

"Sounds like you have a wonderful family," Ron said as dessert was served. "I'd love to hear about your little boy. Rudy, right?"

For the next hour, Mai talked about her son, being careful not to mention Ray, his family, and her miserable life with them.

When the restaurant closed, Ron walked Mai to her car. There, he took her hands in his and she felt the tingle all the way to her chest. "I'll be in town again in a few weeks. I'd like to see you then."

"I'd like that, too."

He bent down and kissed her gently on the cheek.

"I'll get it!" Rudy yelled as he raced to the door.

Mai buckled the belt of the soft knit dress. She brushed her long black hair over her shoulders.

"You must be Rudy," she heard Ron say as she walked to the door.

"Pleased to meet you, Sir," Rudy said, extending a handshake.

Mai had looked forward to this second date since the moment their first date ended. Her mind said to go slow, but her heart told her to run to this man.

"Hi, Ron." She resisted the urge to hug him.

"Mom says maybe tomorrow I can go with you," Rudy piped up.

"I'd like that," Ron said, smiling at MaiLy.

"But tonight you're stuck with me," Gail said as she entered from the kitchen.

After introductions and pleasantries, Ron guided Mai out the door with his arm around her waist. As Mai turned to say good-bye, Gail rolled her eyes, clasped her heart, and dramatically fell into the chair.

During their three-hour dinner, Mai learned more about Ron's family and his work in the electronics industry. He gently coaxed her to talk about herself, but asked no imposing questions. He held her hand across the table as she told stories of her life in Vietnam. She thought she saw tears in his eyes when she recounted her escape on the raft.

"That's probably why I'm such a lousy swimmer today," she said to lighten the mood.

"Do you ever think about going back?" Ron asked. "Or trying to find your family there?"

"I did, as a kid. I even thought I remembered them. But I've given all that up, and to be honest, I'm comfortable with that now. It was all just a daydream."

"There's a lot to be said for daydreams." Ron kissed her fingertips. "Sometimes they come true."

As he walked her to her doorstep, they talked of plans to take Rudy to the Heritage museum the next day. Ron put his arms around her and held her gently. "I can hardly wait 'til tomorrow." Then his lips touched hers in a whisper kiss.

Rudy loved the museum. Intrigued by the Indian artifacts, he had dozens of questions about the Old West. Ron answered them all with detail and animation. MaiLy found the information equally exciting, since she had dropped out of high school before taking American history, a fact she avoided sharing with Ron and her son. The three of them walked hand in hand exploring the Nevada ghost town and outdoor railroad.

Mai hadn't felt this happy since the day Rudy was born
- -when she had kissed and cradled her new life.

At the day's end, she and Ron read Rudy his nightly
bedtime story. Ron looked at his watch. "I'd better get
going. My flight leaves in an hour. I booked a Red-eye so I
could spend the whole day with you."

She walked with him to the door. He cupped her chin
in his hands and kissed her tenderly.

He cared for her.

She felt it in his touch.

Ron's visits became more frequent. He admitted that
not only business, but also now pleasure called him back
often.

Mai nestled next to him, with his arms around her, as
the video movie ended. He turned her toward him and they
shared a long lingering kiss. With warmth and tenderness,
his fingers brushed her cheeks, her forehead, her chin. "I
love you, MaiLy." The love in his eyes moved her heart to
skip a beat.

"Oh, Ron," she whispered. "You don't know me well
enough to love me."

"I know all I need to." He kissed her again.

She pushed away, slowly. "There's so much you don't
know." Then, as if making a cleansing confession, the
words tumbled out. For an hour, she swallowed back tears
and told him about the stealing, the drugs, the relationship
with Ray, everything. Ron's eyes never left hers as he
listened, intent on every word. She finished with, "See? I'm
not who you think I am."

"No," he said, "you're not." He cradled her tenderly
against him. "You're even more." He kissed the tears from
one eye, then the other. "And I love you even more deeply,
if that's possible."

"And I love you," she said softly.

It was the first time she had spoken those words.

Mai adjusted her veil and smoothed the white lace. Her eyes met Ron's loving gaze as he stood nervously at the end of the aisle. His smile grew even wider.

"This is like a daydream," she whispered to herself.

Rudy brushed the dust off the knees of his suit. Thunder rumbled and he pushed open the heavy church door, saying, "Too bad it had to rain on our wedding day."

"It doesn't matter, son," she said out loud. "Nothing can dampen our happiness now. I promise."

"And a promise is a promise," Rudy recited.

He pushed the door open farther. "Cool! Mom! Look at this!"

She held his hand and gazed out the door.

A brilliant rainbow arched above them.

"Yes, a promise is a promise."

Epilog

San Francisco, November 1994

Mai set the dishes on the dining room table. Soon Ron and Rudy would be home from the baseball game and supper would be ready.

The phone rang.

"MaiLy! This is Mom and Dad! We're calling from Dalat! We're on a speaker phone."

Mai had received several postcards from them during their trip to India and Vietnam. They had never phoned from a trip before.

"We found her!" Connie shouted.

"What?"

Pete's voice said clearly, "MaiLy, we found your birth mom."

Mai eased into a dining room chair. Her baby stirred inside her. "What are you talking about?"

"Well," Connie's voice bubbled. "Let's start from the beginning. When we finished business in Saigon, we were supposed to hurry to India, but because of a feared plague outbreak there, we had to stay in Vietnam longer. On a lark, we decided to go to Dalat so Dad could show me where he was stationed and where he found you at Domani de Marie. Before heading out, we went to the Mother House in Saigon, and guess who was there?"

"Sister Chantel!" Pete said. "She is so old and frail, but still looks the same. She's got to be 90 and still directs a preschool there. We showed her your photo and she recognized you!"

Connie broke in. "I know a little French and, even though it's rusty, I understood when she said she always wondered what happened to you. We asked her again,

246

MaiLy, just to be certain. She told us you were abandoned at the orphanage gate and had no family."

Pete jumped in. "So we rented a car and drove four and a half hours to Dalat. It was beautiful. Still surrounded by plantations. We found the lake in the middle of town where we took our paddleboat ride, then found where I had lived. The people let us in and I showed Mom where I wrote her all the letters- - where I sat when I learned Marcie was born, and where I wrote her when I found you." He paused.

"Then," it was Connie's voice; "we went to the hotel and hired an interpreter to come with us to Domani de Marie. The orphanage looks pretty run down. We knocked on a door with cobwebs, and a nun came. I showed her your picture. She recognized you, too! She said they were planning to take you to France to be a nun. Then she said, 'Do you want to meet MaiLy's mother?'"

Pete said, "I didn't believe the interpreter when he said that, but sure enough, this nun insisted she knew her. She said this peasant woman brought you to the orphanage when you were two weeks old because she had two other children and was destitute. She knew you wouldn't survive if she kept you. The woman used to volunteer at the orphanage some just to see you. You even went to her house once. She loved you so." His voice broke so Connie finished.

"When she knew Dalat was falling and the children were leaving, she almost came back to get you, but didn't because with her your future would have been as a beggar, she said. She heard about the plane crash, and assumed you were on it. All these years she's wondered if you were alive."

Pete's turn. "She has come back to the orphanage every year for the past 19 years to see if there is any word of you. That's how this nun knows so much about your story. So, the nun told us to come back at 7:00 to meet your birth mother. So we went back to the hotel and paced and worried for a few hours. By the time we went back to the orphanage, we had convinced ourselves that there were lots of MaiLys in Vietnam and they had you mixed up with someone else.

"But when that door opened," Connie blurted, "and we saw this old Vietnamese lady standing there in a scarf, worn dress, and boots. She only had to smile and we knew it was her. Her eyes crinkled the same way yours do when you smile. I hugged her first," Connie's voice quaked. "She has that same funny cry you do."

The phone was quiet a minute, then Connie said, "We held each other, both crying, 'Mai me, Mai me,' meaning, Mai's mother, Mai's mother."

While Connie softly cried, Pete added, "She said, 'these are not tears of sadness, but tears of joy. I gave her birth.

You gave her life.'"

Mai simply whispered, "I knew it!"

About the Author

LeAnn Thieman is a nationally acclaimed professional speaker, author, and nurse who was "accidentally" caught up in the Vietnam Orphan Airlift in 1975.

Her first book, *This Must Be My Brother,* details her daring adventure of helping to rescue 300 babies as Saigon was falling to the Communists. An ordinary person, she struggled through extraordinary circumstances and found the courage to succeed.

On the 25th Anniversary of Operation Babylift, former President Gerald Ford asked to meet her. *Newsweek Magazine* featured LeAnn and her incredible story in its *Voices of the Century* issue.

Today, as a renowned motivational speaker, she shares life-changing lessons learned from her Airlift experience. Believing we all have individual "war zones," LeAnn inspires audiences to balance their lives, truly live their priorities and make a difference in the world.

After her Airlift story was featured in *Chicken Soup for the Mother's Soul*, LeAnn became one of Chicken Soup's most prolific writers, with stories in eight more Chicken Soup books. She was then invited to co-author *Chicken Soup for the Nurse's Soul, Chicken Soup for the Christian Woman's Soul* and *Chicken Soup for the Caregiver's Soul.*

LeAnn and Mark, her husband of thirty-two years, reside in Colorado where they enjoy their "empty nest." Their two daughters, Angela and Christie, and son Mitch have "flown the coop" but are still drawn under their mother's wing when she needs them!

For more information about LeAnn's books and tapes or to schedule her for a presentation, please contact her at:

LeAnn Thieman
6600 Thompson Drive
Fort Collins, CO 80526
1-970-223-1574
www.LeAnnThieman.com
Email LeAnn@LeAnnThieman.com

LeAnn Thieman